THE SALVAGE
OF THE CENTURY

THE SALVAGE
OF THE CENTURY

By Ric Wharton

BEST PUBLISHING COMPANY

ISBN: 0-941332-79-9
Library of Congress catalog card number: 99-63493

Best Publishing Company
www.bestpub.com

TABLE OF CONTENTS

Prologue VII

Chapter 1 My First Salvage Operation 3
Chapter 2 Getting My Feet Wet 7
Chapter 3 Embarking on Our Own 11
Chapter 4 Arctic Convoys of World War II 19
Chapter 5 The Search for the *Edinburgh* 33
Chapter 6 Striking Gold 81
Chapter 7 Our Ship Comes In 107
Chapter 8 Sailing in Other Waters 119
Chapter 9 The History of the *Conception* 135
Chapter 10 Returning to the *Edinburgh* 145

Epilogue 163

Appendix 1 Atmospheres of Pressure 167
Appendix 2 Helium 169
Appendix 3 Salvage Documents 171
Appendix 4 Salvage Documents 179
Appendix 5 Salvage Documents 187

Acknowledgments 195

References 197

Biography 198

THE SALVAGE
OF THE CENTURY

PROLOGUE

It was April 28, 1942. His Majesty's Heavy Cruiser HMS *Edinburgh* lay restlessly at anchor in the Kola Inlet at Murmansk in the Barents Sea. It was bitterly cold in the Arctic half light and a thin covering of snow lay on her decks. Her captain, Hugh Faulkner, stood on the bridge muffled in his dufflecoat, eager to be away.

He had successfully escorted the outbound convoy code-named PQ 14 from the west coast of Scotland to Murmansk with the loss of only one of the convoy's cargo ships. His principal task was complete. Thirteen fully laden merchantmen had arrived in Russia to help Stalin keep the Germans from the gates of Moscow. More importantly, these supplies would help the Russians tie the Germans down in the east and dramatically reduce the risk of an invasion of mainland Britain.

opp. page: HMS Edinburgh *on convoy duty (Photo courtesy of the Imperial War Museum)*

While he should have been well pleased with his efforts, Captain Faulkner was not a happy man. A cruiser's place was on the high seas, not anchored in confined waters and a sitting duck for marauding bombers from the Luftwaffe bases in northern Norway. The front line was uncomfortably close; at night, flashes of gunfire could be seen.

Faulkner was a firm, but popular, captain, much respected by his crew. To his great discomfort he had Rear-Admiral Stuart Bonham-Carter on board. No naval captain ever likes having an admiral on board to second guess his every move and lord it over him, particularly one such as Bonham-Carter, who was portly, pompous, and not very loveable.

Faulkner fretted about Russian inefficiency and interminable delays in unloading the merchantmen and making ready for the return voyage. Some ships would carry timber, but most were empty of ballast. His temper had not improved when the Royal Naval Mission at nearby Polyarnoe informed him that he was to carry back five and a half tons of gold bullion as Russian payment to America for the war materials that he had just delivered. With his Executive Officer, Commander Jefferies, Faulkner developed a plan to stow the gold in the cruiser's bomb room, deep in the bowels of the ship where the extra weight would not affect her stability.

The gold was to have been carried aboard at night in complete secrecy. Unfortunately, a crate was dropped and its contents spilled out onto the deck, allowing the crew to see its contents. Despite Commander Jefferies' efforts to swear the men in the loading party to secrecy, rumours about the gold spread through the ship like an oil fire. The men convinced themselves that the Germans knew about the secret cargo and would make a supreme effort to sink them.

Privately, Faulkner had some sympathy for this view. He had no faith in Soviet security. He thought it very likely that the Germans would know about the gold and be even more interested in the *Edinburgh*. What Faulkner did not confide in his crew was that on the return journey the U-boats were disinclined to run the gauntlet of the dreaded destroyers to expend an expensive torpedo on an empty merchant ship that America could replace at the rate of one a day. He knew that all the might of the German forces in the area would be directed against the *Edinburgh*.

Captain Faulkner breathed a sigh of relief later that day when the *Edinburgh* finally managed to shepherd her fleet of empty merchantmen out of the Kola Inlet, and into the Barents Sea. He was still grumpy, but he was back at sea where he and his ship belonged. He called for full speed and zig-zagged north at 33 knots. The crew began to

relax and resume their normal seagoing routine. They were going home, and not a moment too soon. The weather was intermittently overcast with clear spells. Faulkner's greatest concern was the Luftwaffe bombers based in northern Norway. If they found him in a clear spell, they would harry him to the death. To increase his chances, he elected to steer north toward the polar ice cap. This would put the *Edinburgh* at the far edge of the Luftwaffe bomber range and severely limit the time they could search for the cruiser.

By the morning of Thursday, April 30, the *Edinburgh* was some 250 miles north west of Murmansk in moderate seas and good visibility. There was no sign of the enemy and the crew's confidence was increasing by the hour. The bulky figure of Bonham-Carter had joined Faulkner on the bridge. Around his neck he carried a Brownie box camera his wife had given him. He told Faulkner that on the next leg of the zig-zag he would like to go up to the edge of the ice pack to take some photos for his wife.

"I would not advise it, sir," said Faulkner. "The U-boats tend to hang about under the edge of the ice waiting for us."

"Nonsense," said Bonham-Carter. "They will never get a shot at us at this speed."

Admiral Bonham-Carter (right) and Captain Faulkner on the bridge. (Photo courtesy of the Imperial War Museum)

At the edge of the ice pack, U 456 waited. Kapitan Max Teichert, the sub commander, looked through his periscope and could not believe his eyes.

Suddenly the ASDIC room called the bridge to report a contact on the starboard bow in the direction of the ice cap. "We had better leave, sir," said Faulkner. "We are picking up a contact on the starboard bow."

"Nonsense," said Bonham-Carter. "It will just be a reflection off the ice."

At 1120 a.m. Kapitan Teichert wrote in his log book, "Signal 1142/701 Most Urgent:- square 5582, cruiser type "Belfast" on westerly course at high speed, zig-zagging sharply." Teichert shadowed her and manoeuvred for position.

Even as Faulkner tried to make Bonham-Carter realise that the ship was in danger, Teichert entered in his log: "Square 5519 AC, wind NW force 6-7, Sea 5-6, visibility 8 miles. Salvo of three torpedoes from tubes 1,2 and 4. Range 1000 metres, angle on bow 60, torpedo speed 30 knots, torpedo depth setting 4 metres, angular spacing 4, point of aim forward funnel."

Damaged decking at the stern (Photo courtesy of the Imperial War Museum)

Lookouts on the *Edinburgh's* bridge spotted the telltale wake of the torpedoes and sounded the alarm, but it was too late. The first torpedo struck under the bridge on the starboard side. A massive explosion shook the ship, one survivor said, "as if someone held it in a giant hand and shook it." Seconds later another massive explosion at the stern slowed the ship dramatically. The *Edinburgh* veered to starboard and took on an immediate list.

There was a momentary silence on the bridge. The helmsman was shocked to hear Faulkner vehemently say to Bonham-Carter, "You fucking bastard, look what you've done to my ship!"

Discipline and emergency procedures took over, and this incident was never mentioned again. However, I suspect it may have been the reason Faulkner was not awarded the D.S.O. he so richly deserved for his part in the action that followed.

The mood in the conning tower of U 456 was dramatically different. An elated Max Teichert wrote in his log: "2 explosions in quick succession, running time 80 seconds, distance 1200 metres, boat dips." This was a great achievement for a lone U-boat and Teichert received his Iron Cross personally from Grand Admiral Doenitz.

Although the second torpedo inflicted the most telling damage, it was the first that caused mayhem, destruction, and death below decks. It struck the lower sheet of armour plating on the starboard side and burst through into the furnace fuel-oil tank, leaving a hole big enough to drive a bus through. The fuel tank was nearly full and the incompressible fuel transmitted the full force of the explosion into the heart of the ship. A small arms magazine and a store room were directly in the path of the torpedo. They shattered and the explosion of water and oil burst up into the seamen's and stoker's mess deck directly above. Off-duty sailors were brewing tea, making toast, and relaxing with their shipmates. The lucky ones fought their way through the flames and debris and climbed up out of the hatchways before these had to be dogged down to save the ship. In some compartments hatches were secured before the crew could escape. Those unfortunates had to be left to asphyxiate.

With the list to starboard already at 7 degrees, Faulkner fired off all the starboard torpedoes to lighten that side of the ship. All non-essential crew rushed to the port side to help right the dangerous list.

For those in the machinery room directly above the fuel tank, death was instantaneous. The force of the explosion, taking the path of least resistance, burst up through the deck, killing everyone in the room. Their bodies, together with machinery and compressors, fell back into the fuel tank.

While damage-control parties struggled to stem the flooding and rescue survivors, Faulkner checked with the engine room and was relieved to learn that all four engines were operating normally. This would not last. It took longer to ascertain the extent of damage to the stern. The second torpedo had struck the crippling blow, aft of the auxiliary propellers and forward of the main propellers and the rudders. Again taking the line of least resistance, the force of this explosion lifted the after deck and bent it over the barrels of "Y" turret, putting it, and "X" turret, out of action.

Damage control parties rushed to shore up the weakened bulkheads with timbers. As they worked, they could hear ominous rending noises; shortly after, the complete stern, with both rudders and main propellers, would break away and sink.

On the bridge, Faulkner and Bonham-Carter could not understand why the

U-boat had not delivered the coup de grace. The convoy, with its escorting destroyers, was miles behind. U 456 had a clear field of action with the *Edinburgh* out of control and virtually dead in the water. Below decks, the crew ballasted compartments on the port side of the ship to correct the starboard list. They were just achieving this when the stern broke off completely. Without that weight, the ship settled some 8 feet at the bow. Eventually, with further ballasting, they got the vessel back onto an even keel, although she now sat some 10 feet lower in the water.

With the damage under control and darkness falling, Faulkner took stock of his position. He did not have an accurate tally of the dead and missing. Two more days would pass before he was able to confirm that he had lost a total of 57 officers and men from his total complement of some 850. He had both auxiliary engines operational and could steam a very erratic course at about 8 knots. At that speed it would take him more than 30 hours to get back to Murmansk, during which time he would be at the mercy of German submarines, aircraft, and surface vessels. His "A" and "B" 6-inch turrets were operational, but his radar fire director was out of action. All his anti-aircraft guns were operational, so he would fight on and head back for Murmansk. Behind them six destroyers escorted the convoy of empty merchantmen: the

Foresight, Forester, Amazon, Bulldog, Beagle and *Beverly*. Two Russian destroyers, the *Gremyaschi* and the *Sokrushitelni*, were under orders to escort the convoy as far as 30 degrees east and then return to Murmansk. The explosions of the torpedoes that had crippled the *Edinburgh* had been seen from the convoy. The *Forester* and *Foresight* detached themselves at full speed to render assistance. They were joined shortly by the *Gremyaschi* and the *Sokrushitelni*. The fear of a U-boat attack diminished with four powerful destroyers forming a screen around the crippled *Edinburgh*.

Meanwhile, Teichert's signal prompted a rapid response. More U-boats were dispatched from the German naval base at Narvik. From Kirkenes, three destroyers were dispatched to engage the *Edinburgh*. The Z 24, Z 25, and the *Hermann Shoemann* posed a more serious threat to the *Edinburgh* than the additional U-boats. The German destroyers got underway at 0100 on May 1 to intercept the *Edinburgh*.

On board the *Edinburgh*, the crew set about the Herculean task of getting the ship and its precious cargo back to Murmansk. Snow started falling and visibility decreased dramatically in the squalls. In Murmansk, frantic activity was underway to send assistance to the *Edinburgh*. Four British minesweepers, the *Harrier, Hussar, Gossamer,* and *Niger* and two Russian vessels, a tugboat and an escort, left Murmansk in search of the *Edinburgh.*

As the rest of the convoy made its escape northwest toward Iceland, shepherded by the destroyers, the rescue of the *Edinburgh* began. Captain Faulkner and his crew were having extreme difficulty steering a straight line. With no rudders and only its auxiliary screws to manoeuver, in one hour alone the bridge had given 64 commands to just one of the engines. Progress was slow and erratic.

To speed progress, the *Forester* took the *Edinburgh* in tow. With her bow down and deep in the water, the *Edinburgh* would not respond and continually broke the tow line. With an enterprising change of tactics, the *Edinburgh* took the *Foresight* in tow to act as a drogue to keep her headed on course. That way, the auxiliary engines could run at cruise speed while the *Forester*, using her steering, pulled the *Edinburgh* round onto the right heading. This unorthodox procedure worked while the *Foresight* and the Russian destroyers provided the U-boat screen. Throughout the night, they made erratic progress back toward Murmansk at about three knots.

At 0600 on May 1, the Russian destroyers announced they were low on fuel and would have to return immediately to Murmansk to refuel. This was a crushing blow. To the British, it was inconceivable that both destroyers would run low on fuel at the same time. Why hadn't the Russians refuelled before sailing out to render assistance? It transpired that the reason had more to do with the May Day celebrations scheduled for that evening, and was to cause a diplomatic incident to contribute to a simmering resentment between the Allies.

With the departure of the Russian destroyers, Faulkner had inadequate protection against U-boat attack. He cast off the *Foresight* so that he would have a minimum of two screening destroyers. All he could now do was to try to steer the *Edinburgh* as before, and wait for the arrival of the Russian tug.

Meanwhile, the Germans were starting to harass the tail-end of convoy QP 11, although Luftwaffe torpedoes failed to cause any damage. Mid-morning on May 1, the *Beverly*, on the port side of the convoy, sighted the three German destroyers. In a brief engagement, *Amazon* was damaged and a Russian straggler was torpedoed and sunk. The German destroyers made five attempts to attack the convoy and were driven off each time by the British destroyer screen. Under a smokescreen, the three German destroyers headed off to intercept the *Edinburgh.* The U-boats continued unsuccessfully to attack the destroyer escort. They broke off the engagement and abandoned the convoy to continue its journey homeward with no further losses.

At 1800 on May 1, the minesweepers arrived, accompanied by the Russian tug and the *Rubin*. The tug proved too small to tow the *Edinburgh*, so it was used for steering on the starboard bow with the *Gossamer* acting as a drag on the port stern. Through the night, the *Edinburgh* limped toward Murmansk. Every mile brought her and her escorts nearer to safety and morale on the ship was beginning to rise. Faulkner estimated that the Russian destroyers had had time to refuel and were expected back at any minute to escort *Edinburgh* the final miles to safety. But they did not arrive. It would seem that the aftermath of the May Day celebrations precluded an early start. With lame excuses of engine trouble, the Russians did not leave Murmansk until 0800 that morning, presumably after sobering up. They would be far too late to render any assistance.

At 0630 on May 2, the *Hussar* sighted the three German destroyers. They were heavily armed with 5.9- and 5-inch guns. The minesweepers each had single, 4-inch guns. *Hussar* alerted the *Edinburgh* and opened fire. The crew on board the *Edinburgh* had been at action stations all night, but now Lieutenant Commander Howe rushed to the forward turrets. With only verbal communications available, Faulkner leaned over the bridge rail and instructed Howe

to engage the enemy. He ordered his crew to cast off her drag and her tow. At a full speed of about seven knots, the *Edinburgh* circled erratically to port. Lieutenant Commander Howe fired whenever he could bring the guns to bear. Visibility varied. The German ships frequently disappeared into the mist. After two broadsides, Howe managed to score a direct hit on the *Hermann Shoemann*. The destroyer immediately went dead in the water and began to list. Lt. Commander Howe was subsequently awarded a well-deserved Distinguished Service Cross for this incredible feat of naval gunnery.

Meanwhile, the *Forester* and *Foresight* engaged the enemy destroyers at close range. While her captain leaned over the bridge railing shouting encouragement to the forward gun crew, the *Forester* received a direct hit at the base of the bridge. The captain was killed along with 22 others of his crew, and the ship stopped. The *Foresight* was hit five times and also brought to a halt.

Providentially, Z 24 and Z 25 stopped to pick up survivors from the *Hermann Shoemann*. This gave the crews of the *Forester* and the *Foresight* time to make temporary repairs and get underway again.

The brave little minesweepers now took up the fight. Although hopelessly

Survivors being loaded onto HMS Harrier. *(Photo courtesy of the Imperial War Museum)*

out-gunned, they attacked the enemy head-on at full speed. In the poor visibility, the Germans actually thought they were up against a force of five destroyers. With survivors from the *Herman Shoemann* the Z 24 and Z 25 returned to the fray. Z 24 now fired a fan of three torpedoes at the *Edinburgh*. Seeing them coming, Faulkner tried to turn his bow toward them to allow the torpedoes to pass down either side of the vessel. With so little power, the *Edinburgh's* response was too slow and, heeling hard to port, she took a torpedo

hit full on the port side and opposite the site of the first torpedo hit. The colossal impact sent water spraying over the bridge. Deck plates peeled up behind the bridge.

Rear Admiral Bonham-Carter was convinced the *Edinburgh* was "open from side to side" and "her back was broken." He gave the order to abandon ship. The *Gossamer* took off 400 survivors and the *Harrier* 350. Interestingly, a Russian vessel rammed into the *Harrier* while the crew was loading survivors (a letter of apology from the Russian commander was later sent). The *Edinburgh* doggedly refused to sink. Many of her crew wanted to reboard her and continue the fight. Not wanting to leave the ship to the enemy, Bonham-Carter ordered the *Foresight* to put a torpedo into her engine room to sink her. The proud ship sank quickly, rolling to port and sinking stern first. She paused with just her bows showing, "curtsied" and disappeared below the waves. She took with her two officers and 55 men who had given their lives in that gallant struggle.

The Germans, still thinking that they were up against a force of five destroyers, retreated under smoke. Aboard the minesweepers the survivors, now crammed shoulder-to-shoulder, toasted the *Edinburgh* with a full mug of navy rum each.

So ended one of the most gallant and poorly recorded naval actions of World War II. The recriminations, however, would ring on. As Captain Faulkner set about writing his letters of condolence to the relatives of the dead, a signal from Admiralty asked if the gold had been saved. Bonham-Carter brusquely replied that the gold had been in a compartment flooded by the first torpedo.

Admiral Bevan, based in Murmansk, wrote a report on the sinking that was a scathing indictment of the behaviour of the two Russian destroyers; he

A letter of apology from the Russian commander to the Harrier.

maintained that they were largely to blame for the ultimate loss of the *Edinburgh*. For their part, the Russians fought back. Admiral Golovko, the senior Russian officer in Murmansk, carried out his own inquiry into the sinking; he was extremely critical of Bonham-Carter for giving the order to abandon ship when the vessel was not in sinking condition and could have fought on.

After a long and uncomfortable wait in Murmansk, Bonham-Carter raised his ill-fated flag again on HMS *Trinidad*, a heavy cruiser that had been severely damaged while escorting the outbound convoy PQ 13. Bonham-Carter had to wait while repairs were completed in drydock, using plating that the *Edinburgh* had carried out specially from the UK because none had been available in Russia. Captain Faulkner was also on board, with many of the *Edinburgh* survivors who were taking the place of crew members lost on its outward trip. The Trinidad also carried the sick and wounded from the *Edinburgh.* The Germans, expecting her departure, harried and bombed the *Trinidad* incessantly for three days, sinking her with great loss of life and leaving Faulkner and Bonham-Carter to find their way home on smaller escorts. Bonham-Carter's reputation took a bit of a downturn after losing two ships, and his sailors began to refer to their life jackets as "Bonhams."

The loss of two capital ships in such a short space of time was a serious blow to the beleaguered Churchill and forced him to issue orders severely restricting any vessel larger than a destroyer from sailing farther than 4 degrees east in support of the Arctic convoys.

Reading the accounts now, I find it hard to understand the bad grace with which the Russians accepted the vital assistance that Britain so selflessly gave them to save their country from German domination. America may have provided the war materials from their factories (for payment in gold), but it was British warships and British lives that were expended to deliver it at a time when Britain stood in great peril.

Britain undoubtedly deserved more gratitude and support from the Russians. As for the actions of Bonham-Carter, from our perspective 40 years later and knowing what we know now, they raise many questions. But what right have I, or anyone else, to question the actions of brave men in such appalling circumstances so far from home? Still, I can't help but wonder what the outcome might have been if Faulkner had been in sole command of his ship.

In any event, Bonham-Carter was knighted, and retired as a full admiral in 1944. Faulkner finally received his long overdue DSO in late 1942 and would retire as a rear admiral in 1952.

In the meantime, the gold bullion lay forgotten in the fog of war. The insurance monies paid off; the gold was a total loss and beyond the reach of man and technology. But future events, unforeseen at that time, would one day bring together the technology and the men who could use it. By what quirk of fate was it to be me who was to lead those men?

MY FIRST

SALVAGE OPERATION

CHAPTER 1

I sank through the crystal clear waters of the Mediterranean, my pulse racing with excitement and suppressed fear. After weeks of anticipation and doubt, I was finally exploring the newly discovered Roman shipwreck off the village of Zlendi on the Island of Gozo. The wreck had recently been seen by Royal Air Force divers based at Luqua airfield on nearby Malta.

The year was 1966. Having successfully completed my undergraduate degree in Civil Engineering at Imperial College in London, I had worked for a year in industry and returned to Imperial to obtain a Master's Degree in Business.

In all honesty, the real reason I returned was to pursue my passion for diving. As a raw undergraduate at the age of 18, I had seen a notice encouraging new undergraduates to join the newly formed diving club.

opp. page: HMS Edinburgh *in quieter days. (Photo courtesy of the Imperial War Museum)*

Basic training was in the Hammersmith baths in London, but our first taste of real diving was in the cold, murky waters of Stoney Cove in Leicestershire. 1963 was very early in the evolution of scuba diving. We were all inspired by Cousteau, but lacked the comfortable environment of the Mediterranean Sea.

My first interest in diving had indeed been aroused by Cousteau's "The Living Sea." I received this film as a prize at St. Albans School at the age of 16. This would turn out to be my only brush with stardom in a school career that developed into a full-scale battle of wits between myself and the demoralised teaching staff.

Our diving equipment was rudimentary even by the standards of the day. Our cylinders were army surplus gas tanks, our regulators were the original Cousteau/Gargin designed two-stage models with convoluted hoses and our diving suits were homemade, cut against paper patterns and glued together.

My "fond" memories of the Stoney Cove dives are that, as soon as you entered the water, the suit came unstuck at the crotch or the armpit. This let in so much cold water that the well-tried divers' central heating systems were completely inadequate unless we had at least six pints of beer the previous night.

Unfortunately, we soon found that our "heating solution" rotted the glue even more quickly and the suits started to fall to pieces.

The dive at Zlendi was the culmination of all our training and our first truly deep dive. From Stoney Cove, we had progressed to sea dives on the South Coast. From there, we would venture to Guernsey, courtesy of one of the club founders, Roger Wiley, whose father rashly let us borrow his motor yacht on regular weekends to get there.

That summer, we were all in Malta on a diving expedition accompanied by my future wife, Jackie. Our confidence was immediately boosted by the warm, clear water. We soon began to hear rumours that the RAF diving club had seen an amphora wreck on the outer edge of the submerged reef that runs out from the old crusader watch tower at Zlendi. The wreck was reported to be over 61 metres (200 feet) down and loaded with amphora. Then, as now, any full-blooded diver is on the warpath at the mention of amphorae.

Armed with an overabundance of confidence and our rudimentary equipment, we set out for Zlendi, little more than a hamlet in those days. We decided that two of us would dive the wreck while one waited at 30 metres (100 feet) to keep watch over the divers at the bottom. We operated from a Zodiac inflatable with 9 metres (30 feet) of decompression line hung over the side, weighted with a stone.

Roger Wiley and I were to go to the bottom while Jackie was left to wait apprehensively in the Zodiac. We calculated from the Royal Navy decompression tables that we could spend 11 minutes on the bottom and decompress for 20 minutes at 30 feet. We had spare air tanks and regulators hanging from the decompression line in case we appeared to run low.

At about 30 metres (100 feet) down we came to the top of the reef and saw the seabed below us at the base of the submerged cliff. It became noticeably colder, which added to the sense of isolation. The compressed air began to taste and sound metallic. With a wave to our watcher who was to stay there, Roger and I headed down. At 55 metres (180 feet) the bottom still seemed a long way away and we began to question ourselves. This was the point of no return; beyond this depth it was too far to make an emergency ascent if a regulator failed. I then spotted the outline of the wreck, lying parallel to the base of the cliff in a white sand bottom, and all doubts disappeared. I looked at my depth gauge — 75 metres (245 feet) — far too deep. (The legal air diving limit is now 50 metres [165 feet]).

As I knelt on the bottom at one end of the wreck, I saw an earthenware bowl about 15 inches in diameter partially buried in the sand. I pulled it excitedly from the sand. I had my first artifact from an ancient Roman wreck. The bowl had a hole in it and I remember slipping it over my arm as I moved further along the wreck, where I found the neck and handles of an amphora and quickly grabbed them.

That was when I noticed rows and rows of humps in the sand on each side of the wreck. Feeling through the sand, I realised that this was the vessel's cargo of amphorae, still in their original rows.

I stood astride, panting from the exertion, and hauled a pristine amphora from its sandy grave, the first human hand to touch it for some 1,700 years. I could already see it in a black wrought iron stand complete with a shining brass plate, adorning my sitting room. Little did I know, drunk as I was with nitrogen narcosis, that it would be many years before that dream would be fulfilled.

I glanced at my watch and realised my 10 minutes were up and it was time to go. I struck out for the surface clutching my prizes. Moments later, my pulse racing, I was breathing faster than my regulator could supply the air but my flippers were still on the bottom. Fortunately, through the narcotic haze, I realised that I was too heavy to swim to the surface. Reluctantly, I let go the amphora neck and tried again. Finally, on the point of blacking out, and with my feet still in the sand, I was forced to let go of the complete amphora.

To this day, I can still see my fireside ornament falling gently back onto the seabed as I rose toward the surface. As I approached the surface, my panic subsided, I regained control of my breathing, and I sobered up from my nitrogen narcotic stupor. At 45 metres (150 feet) I caught sight of the minder waiting to guide me back to the decompression line. It was then my sanity returned. I realised (to my lasting shame) that in the heat of the moment I had completely forgotten my partner, Roger, and hadn't the vaguest idea where he was.

Relief flooded through me as I saw him above, already on the decompression line. Images of how I would have explained his early demise to his distraught parents flashed through my mind. I suspect, if the truth were known, he probably was thinking the same about me.

Five minutes into the decompression Roger pointed quizzically to my "armband" and I remembered that I still had the bowl. Now, nearly 30 years later, it has pride of place in our lounge and serves to remind me of the sheer stupidity of that, my first-ever salvage dive, which could so easily have been my last.

Little did I know that 16 hectic years later, this passion for diving was to lead me to carry out the greatest and most successful salvage of the twentieth century.

GETTING
MY FEET WET

CHAPTER 2

It was the Zlendi dive that did the damage and set me on the road to a career in diving and salvage. I became a Maritime Civil Engineer, designing and building the lifeboat station at Trevose Head in Cornwall for the RNLI. From there, I went on to build sea defences and harbour installations, always managing to keep myself near the sea, and diving regularly.

After five years together, I married Jackie and we set up a home in London in 1969. At the same time, I abandoned civil engineering for good and joined the oilfield diving industry. I was promptly sent to Kharg Island in the Arabian Gulf to install an offshore loading terminal. I spent three and a half months living in squalor on a 150-foot-long barge and learned the diving business very quickly.

By the mid-sixties commercial diving had moved away from the ubiquitous

opp. page: The Dammtor *on location April 1981. (Photo by M. Stewart)*

bronze hard helmet and heavy, leaden boots. By this time, the divers were using rubber dry suits with light-weight helmets, but they were still relying on air as the breathing medium. This effectively limited the maximum depth of divers to 60 to 90 metres (200 to 300 feet). (See Appendix Technical 1) This was the major constraint that the commercial diving industry was wrestling with in the late sixties when the North Sea was in its infancy, and the reason the *Edinburgh* lay undisturbed, beyond the wildest dreams of salvage divers.

After the Arabian Gulf, I went to work for Comex as Managing Director of their new UK company, Comex Diving Ltd. This was 1970 and the North Sea Oil Boom was just starting. In these early days, the contractual and management effort was based in Great Yarmouth on the coast of Norfolk in the southern sector of the North Sea. Phillips Petroleum was just discovering the massive Ekofisk oil field with the "Gulftide" jack-up drilling rig. British Petroleum was about to hire the revolutionary new semi-submersible floating drilling rig "Sea Quest" that was to discover the giant Forties field, and prove that the North Sea was one of the world's great oil fields.

Comex was just getting off the ground and was an innovative French diving company based in Marseilles. It was owned and run by a brilliant French engineer, Henri Delauze, who has probably contributed more to the development of the diving industry than any other individual. Henri was, and still is, a wreck diver at heart, but unfortunately he has yet to find the "big one" that he really deserves.

When I took over Comex Diving, its annual turnover was about £150,000. When I left in 1976 to set up my own firm, the turnover had risen to £25,000,000. That hectic period saw not only the technical development of deep diving techniques, but also their application in the hostile environment of the North Sea.

I had no idea, as we rode the crest of that technological wave as precariously balanced as a surfer, that it was that very technology which was to bring the *Edinburgh* into the reach of man. It was no small amount of luck that I was to be one of those men.

In those early days of the seventies, before the legal limit was set at 50 metres (165 feet) for air diving, the oil companies were moving into deeper and deeper water. They expected the diving contractors to have the equipment, technology, and trained personnel to support them. The market was dominated by American contractors from the Gulf of Mexico who were trying to extrapolate their air-diving technology to the North Sea environment. Henri Delauze and Comex were strides ahead of the Americans, thanks to

Henri's personal foresight. He had persuaded the French government to fund his research into deep diving using mixtures of helium and oxygen. (See Appendix Technical 2)

When I worked in the Arabian Gulf in 1970, the divers were still using air at 55 metres (180 feet) and taking lengthy decompression stops at the stern of the barge under the diving ladder. This area was illuminated at night by a powerful lamp on the crane boom above it. This light tended to attract fish, and, of course, several sharks.

To make matters worse, the local crew used to fish off the barge when they were off duty. That, added to all the raw sewage and garbage that was discharged directly from the barge, made it a popular haven for sharks.

We were soon adopted by a school of large tiger sharks who became very interested in the divers hanging on the decompression line. To them, we must have looked like shark-sized bait on a large fishing line.

They began constantly circling the divers from about 6 metres (20 feet) away, staring at them with unwavering eyes (sharks don't blink). Finally, the inevitable happened. One night a tiger shark suddenly turned and darted at a diver, brushing over the top of his head. The diver promptly surfaced like a Polaris Missile. "Fuck the decompression," he said. "I'm not staying in there."

We had to recompress him in a surface chamber, and carry out a much longer decompression. Needless to say, the divers immediately went on strike. My initial reaction was to go in myself and show them that it was safe. Fortunately, that impulse lasted about half a second.

We sat idle for two days while the school of tiger sharks cruised around the barge, waiting for the crumbs from our table (and possibly an entree of a diver). Finally, the Iranian cook, in a mixture of Farsi and broken English, suggested that we catch one, cut it up, and put it back in the water. He said the other sharks would then go away.

I did not believe a word of it but the prospect of free game fishing was better that sitting around doing nothing. We made a large hook from a length of half-inch reinforcing bar, baited it with a leg of pork from the freezer, and used a five-litre olive oil tin as a float.

We rigged this on a heavy rope and fished from a small supply boat that ran the barge's anchors. After about 10 minutes, we hooked a tiger shark 4 metres (12 feet) long. We lifted it on board with the cargo crane, cut it up in sections, and tipped it overboard. I expected to see a feeding frenzy from the other sharks, but nothing happened. We followed the remains for three hours as the pieces drifted away without so much as a ripple on the surface.

To my amazement, we never saw another tiger shark for the rest of the job.

EMBARKING
ON OUR OWN

CHAPTER 3

In the rapidly changing world of high technology, I was able to rely on the research work of our head office at Marseilles to develop better technological advances in the diving field. It was my job, as managing director of Comex in the UK, to apply this new technology to the emerging frontier oil fields of the North Sea. Unbeknownst to me in those frenetic days, the very technology I was developing was to lead me directly to HMS *Edinburgh* and the greatest treasure ever to be recovered by divers.

At Comex we built bell diving systems where the diving bell locked onto a chamber on the surface. The divers used a heliox mixture and decompressed as soon as they locked back into the chamber on deck. This came to be known as "bounce diving."

The next step in saturation diving required the building of large chamber complexes where the divers could live on deck, at the seabed pressure, and be transported to the seabed in the diving bell for each working shift on the bottom. This way, the divers could live and work for days on end, and decompress on the surface in comfort at the end of the diving program. These techniques were not fully developed until the mid-seventies, and even then the deepest water that we were required to work in was about 137 metres (450 feet).

Once we developed diving systems that negated the need for divers to decompress in the water, other commercial pressures began to build up. Our equipment was large and heavy and took time to install and remove from a construction barge. Furthermore, the diving bells were launched over the side of the barges and their operation was very weather dependent.

Early on, I realized that the market would require dedicated diving-support ships. Comex could never have afforded that level of investment, so I looked around for an adventurous ship owner as a partner.

By extremely good fortune I met John Houlder, who had his own family shipping line "Houlder Brothers." John was, and still is, larger than life, mildly eccentric, and brilliant. He adopted us

opp. page: HMS Belfast *at sea. (Photo courtesy of the Imperial War Museum)*

and I appointed him as chairman of Comex Diving. John unselfishly helped me build up the company, and he was truly a pioneer of the North Sea.

Together we planned the conversion of one of his ore carriers, the *Oregis*, into the North Sea's first dedicated diving-support vessel. The ship was equipped with a revolutionary moonpool, or shaft, in the centre of the vessel. Through this, the diving bell could be lowered in virtually any weather condition.

This single development changed the face of the diving industry. The diving companies now became main contractors working directly for the oil companies, rather than subcontractors working for the American construction companies.

Amid the offshore work, we still found time to chase the salvage rainbow. I knew that, lying somewhere in the waters of the Channel Islands, was one of the most important British Naval wrecks, HMS *Victory*. This ship had 110 bronze cannons which would have been of the finest quality in order to befit its status. This was the predecessor to Nelson's *Victory*. At the time of her loss in 1744, she was the biggest in the world, the flagship of the Royal Navy and, of course, "unsinkable."

This was during the war of "Jenkin's Ear" in the Spanish Peninsula. The war

started when a Spaniard rather unreasonably caused offence by slicing off the ear of one of the British officers, named Jenkins, with his sword. In the war that followed, Admiral Balchen took the *Victory* at the head of a garrison relief fleet to Portugal. This was regarded as a 'milk run' with little danger, and many sons of famous families were on board as midshipmen and junior officers. Altogether there were some 1100 men aboard the *Victory*.

As the fleet returned that autumn they ran into bad weather. This rapidly developed into the worst storm of that century. So severe were the winds that ships at anchor at Portsmouth had their upper yards snapped off. The fleet was dispersed and, after several days, the battered vessels began to limp into port, but there was no sign of the *Victory*. The Admiralty was not unduly concerned about its unsinkable flagship until boats bringing vegetables from the Channel Islands began to report that a large and unidentified ship had been lost there.

At the northwestern tip of the Channel Islands to the west of Alderney lie the Casquets rocks, still feared by sailors to this day. With a tidal rise and fall of 10 metres (33 feet) and currents of up to 9 knots with violent overfalls, these waters are among the most dangerous in the world and are the graveyard of many ships. Already by 1744, there was a rudimentary lighthouse in the

Casquets fired by coal that had to be laboriously carried up the tower by hand. For some inexplicable reason the lighthouse was manned at the time by two French Catholics.

Our research led us to reports by the Lloyds agent in Guernsey to the Admiralty. These reports revealed that, on the night in question, these "ordinary gentlemen," being too lazy to carry up the coals, had failed to light the signal. In addition, they had reported that an unknown ship had stuck on the rocks during the night and fired many signal guns, but by morning there was no sign of her.

Still the Admiralty believed that the *Victory* was just delayed. Then came reports of spars and rigging washed up on the beaches of Normandy. As final and mournful proof, the lid of a midshipman's chest with his name engraved on a brass plate inlet was found when it washed ashore.

The government of the day feared the public reaction to such a catastrophic loss and delayed announcing it for three months. Of the unfortunate crew there was no trace. The sea usually gives up its dead, but all our inquiries could find was a report of one unidentified body being washed up in Sark.

I set up a partnership with Henri Delauze and the Belgian researcher Robert Stenuit to search for the *Victory*.

Robert Stenuit had achieved fame in the sixties by finding the wreck of the *Girona*, a Spanish Armada galleass, on the north coast of Ireland. The wonderful artifacts he recovered are still on display in Belfast.

We also sought the help of two Guernsey divers; Richard Keen, who is the acknowledged expert on wrecks in the Channel Islands, and Mike Rogers, who had been on the trail of the *Victory* for years.

From the facts available, we deduced that she had struck, and stuck on, the Black Rock, just west of the Casquets Rock. She must have been drifting helplessly under bare poles with most of her crew below deck. She must have come off during the night badly holed and, sinking slowly, drifted away, more at the mercy of the tide than the wind.

We started our search by swimming radial lines out from the Black Rock. We had calculated back the times and direction of tides on the night she was lost and were able to direct our search along her presumed final course. Weeks of searching were to no avail, and the wreck of HMS "*Victory*" with its 110 bronze cannons is still a secret of the deep.

A tantalising report in *Blackwoods* magazine later that year gives an account of a passenger boat en route from France to England passing the site of a large shipwreck. It describes a mast and spars floating on the surface, still attached by the rigging to the submerged wreck. Unfortunately, they did not give an accurate position.

We did, however, find the wreck of the South West Region Railway paddle steamer, the *Stella*, that had hit the Casquets in fog while racing a rival steamer. It was sunk at Easter 1895 en route from Weymouth to Guernsey, and 95 lives were lost in the disaster.

We also found the wreck of a privateer called the *Spritely*, and were able to defray some of our costs selling artifacts recovered from it at auction in London.

Richard Keen, while searching for the *Victory*, also found the wreck of the English East Indiaman the *Vallentine* lost off Sark in 1779 on her way back from a four-year voyage to the Far East, laden with porcelain, dyewood for making rouge, and semi-precious stones.

Although the *Victory* has no monetary value, it still attracts me every bit as much as a treasure salvage. One day a fisherman will snag his nets, record the position, and hire a diver to go down for a look. To that diver will fall the honour of finding the most important missing vessel of the Royal Navy. I hope that the honour will fall to Richard Keen and Mike Roger, who

have put so much effort into the search over so many years.

By 1976, I had built Comex Diving up to an annual turnover of £25 million with a commanding share of the North Sea diving market. In the latter years of my time with Comex, Malcolm Williams had worked for me running the UK company while I took responsibility for both UK and Norway. Malcolm is a former colonial policeman and a brilliant and patient administrator. We clearly made a powerful team and decided that it was time we bit the bullet and set off on our own.

In late 1976, we set up Wharton Williams Ltd., and started on our own with one secretary, Pat, and the irrepressible Terry Gosling as our first diving superintendent. Terry suggested as a joke that we should call the company 2W and the name stuck. The company that was to salvage the HMS *Edinburgh* had now been formed and the technology was being rapidly developed. Still, the *Edinburgh* slumbered on in her watery grave, unaware that events were rapidly unfolding that were soon to lead to her discovery and salvage.

As the *Edinburgh* lay waiting for us, Malcolm and I set about building a British diving company with British technology which could take on the French and the Americans in the marketplace. I am an entrepreneur at heart, and was always happiest selling and doing the deals while Malcolm generally stayed at home, sorting out my mistakes and making the deals work.

Malcolm has always erred on the side of caution (which has saved us from a few disasters over the years), while I am pretty headstrong when I get my teeth into something and don't readily let go. We controlled the company 50/50, so we had to agree and always did. I considered it my duty to fire Malcolm up and enthuse him, while he considered that his duty was to slow me down. It was a match made in heaven.

Jackie and I had been trying for several years to acquire a derelict castle nestled in the foothills of the Grampians a few miles outside Aberdeen, in Scotland. The owners were elderly and could not decide whether to part with it. It was sod's law that after trying to buy it for three years, it finally came up one month after we started 2W. That began a do-it-yourself restoration project that was to take three years and every spare evening and weekend Jackie and I had.

In early 1977, I got wind of a big diving contract to be let in New Zealand, so I chased it up and managed to get on the bid list. We were then invited over by the client, Shell, to present our proposal. I flew non-stop London to Los Angeles, and from there non-stop to Auckland where I hired a car and drove the length of the North Island to New Plymouth. More than a little jet-lagged, I duly did my "dog and pony" show, only to be told that they did not want any of the bidders staying in town; we were all to go home and await Shell's decision.

Back I went the same way, arriving in Aberdeen mid-morning UK time. I called in at the office to brief Malcolm. While I was talking to him, a telex came in from Shell "requesting my presence soonest to discuss our proposal." I shot home, packed some clean shirts, kissed the wife hello and good-bye, and shot back to the airport. I did not even see the older kids who were at school. I left immediately for Auckland non-stop again (and all in economy I might add, as we could not afford business class).

My discussions with Shell went well. They said it would take a week or two to get a decision through their partners in the field, and I might as well go home and wait. I smelt blood and refused to leave. Shell got so embarrassed having me hanging around their reception area all day, they finally gave me an office to work in.

It was some six weeks before I got home, but when I did I was armed with a signed contract that was to make us an enormous profit and set 2W on the road to becoming one of the largest diving contractors in the world. We had a turnover of £100 million by the time we eventually sold it.

During those hectic years I missed a lot of my children's growing up, which is the inevitable but high price one pays building up a company. To compensate a bit for these enforced absences, it became a tradition that Malcolm and I brought our older children into the office on Saturday mornings. This was really a clean up time when the phone didn't ring; we could catch up on paper work and quietly plot the downfall of our competitors. I had just about finished my restoration at the castle, but Malcolm had embarked on the renovation of his own; an old farmhouse near the office.

On Saturday morning in 1980, Malcolm and I were doing our usual plotting in my office while the kids terrorised Pat in the general office. Pat came in to announce that Keith Jessop had arrived and wanted to talk to us about a salvage job. Keith is an effervescent, enthusiastic Yorkshireman who had worked for us on and off as a diver, but who tends to rabbit on when he gets the bit between his teeth. Malcolm said "I haven't time to listen to all that bullshit, I've got work to do at home." Before I could protest, he disappeared through the escape door in my office that led directly out to the car park, complete with his share of the kids.

Thank God I didn't do the same! At the end of the job, when we were doling out the money, I reminded Malcolm about that, but he had suffered from total amnesia and quite unreasonably insisted on his full share.

ARCTIC CONVOYS

OF WORLD WAR II

CHAPTER 4

I sat back and listened as Keith's started to tell me the incredible story of HMS *Edinburgh.*

HMS *Edinburgh* was built in the late thirties in the scramble to re-arm Britain for the coming war. She was launched at Wallsend on Tyne in 1938 and commissioned the following year. She was a heavy cruiser of 10,000 tons displacement. Only two of her class were built, the other being HMS *Belfast.* The *Belfast* was badly damaged by a mine early in the war and spent much of the war under repair. She survived and, much to our good luck, is now moored at Tower Bridge as a floating museum. Apart from the addition of a heavy armour skirt, she is virtually identical to the *Edinburgh.*

The *Edinburgh* was one of Britain's major capital ships. With a top speed of 32 knots, she was equipped with four

opp. page: HMS Edinburgh *on convoy duty. (Photo courtesy of the Imperial War Museum)*

turrets each of three 6-inch guns; "A" and "B" turrets at the bow and "X" and "Y" turrets at the stern. Her main armament also included six torpedo launching tubes and 12 anti-aircraft guns. In addition, there was a large aircraft hanger in the base of her bridge that housed four Walrus seaplanes. These were launched over the side with a steam catapult and recovered using a gantry crane. She had a total crew of 850 officers and men.

Her first action came in the first German bombing raid on Britain in October of 1939. She was anchored in the Firth of Forth where both she and the famous Forth bridge were attacked. She escaped lightly with a few men injured from bomb shrapnel. After a short period of patrol work off Norway, she was assigned to convoy escort duty, first in the North Sea, and then on the infamous Malta run. By the start of 1942, she was on escort work on the dreaded Arctic convoys.

When Hitler attacked Russia early on the morning of June 22, 1941, the entire course of the war was changed. Before that, Britain was fighting alone; the Americans were not to join the war until December of that year.

By the end of the first day, the Luftwaffe had destroyed approximately 2,000 Russian aircraft, many still on the ground. The attack was greeted with relief by the beleaguered Churchill.

With typical far-sightedness, he could see that a prolonged campaign in Russia would fatally weaken Germany and remove the threat of an imminent invasion of mainland Britain.

There was massive distrust between Russia and Britain, but Churchill pragmatically set that aside and agreed to help Stalin with war supplies to the extent of our limited ability. When criticised about this decision Churchill replied, "If Hitler invaded Hell I would at least make a favourable reference to the Devil in the House of Commons."

In 1941, Britain was itself in desperate need of resupply and Churchill had already negotiated the Lease Lend deal with Roosevelt that was to provide the material to allow Churchill to "finish the job." Stalin jumped on the band wagon and demanded the same deal. His first request included 20,000 anti-aircraft guns and one million rifles. This was shortly followed by a further demand for a large number of fighters and 3,000 bombers.

In July, Churchill agreed to send some 200 fighters to Russia from Britain's own stocks. British submarines were sent to patrol the Kola Inlet and the approaches to Murmansk. A British Naval Mission was established at Polyarnoe, a Russian naval base close to Murmansk.

This spirit of cooperation did not run to financial trust. The Russians were required to pay for these supplies in hard currency: in their case, this was gold bullion. Stalin's demands rapidly grew to include 30,000 tons of aluminum over the next few months and 400 aircraft and 500 tanks per month. Churchill responded by offering Stalin half of Britain's output of tanks and planes. America was now gearing up its production and, by late 1942, was able to offer Russia and Britain 1,200 tanks per month each, which was a staggering number. All that was now required was to deliver them safely.

The first aircraft were delivered in September 1941, flown off an aircraft carrier to help with the defence of Murmansk that was by then under constant German attack. The scene was now set for the start of the Arctic convoys that were to cost Great Britain a painfully large number of ships and men.

The convoys had a peculiar numbering system. They were designated PQ for outbound trips and QP for return trips. The first outbound convoy PQ 1 left Iceland with 10 ships on September 29, 1941, and arrived safely in Archangel on October 11.

The convoys started in 1941 in an atmosphere of phony war. The Germans were preoccupied with their land campaign and did not seem worried by the convoy activity under their noses. By the end of 1941 nearly 100 ships laden with vital supplies had arrived safely, with the loss of only one merchant vessel and one military escort. Sadly, this success rate was not to last. As the German advance into Russia started to lose momentum, due to the dogged resistance of the Russians fighting on home territory for their motherland, the Germans began to realise that, unless they could stem the flow of supplies, they would be unable to defeat the Russians.

The Arctic convoys started to receive the undivided attention of the German U-boats and surface ships, and the Luftwaffe based in northern Norway. The constant threat of Germany's greatest battleship, the *Tirpitz*, lurking in the northern Norwegian fjords, together with the Luftwaffe bombers based at Kirkenes in northern Norway, served to drive the convoy routes far to the north, and close to the ice cap. The U-boats straddled the convoy routes and lay in wait.

There was also the additional, and often more insidious, enemy — the weather. In those latitudes, arctic lows arrive without notice, bringing gale force winds and mountainous seas. The sea spray freezes on decks and rigging, its weight seriously affecting the stability of a ship. In these awful

conditions, sailors were required to chip off ice formations with axes. High-speed warships are narrow and designed to move fast. It does not take much ice at deck level and higher to make them unstable. The quality of clothing and gloves were barely adequate, and the heating systems of the vessels could not maintain a comfortable temperature with any regularity.

Fear of enemy attack was heightened by the knowledge that immersion in the sea would be fatal unless rescued immediately. Even if you made it to a lifeboat, you would still be at great risk from exposure. The crews in the armed escorts could at least put up a fight, but the unarmed merchantmen were literally sitting ducks. These crews were the unsung heroes of the arctic convoys, particularly those on the oil tankers that could become incendiary bombs when hit by a torpedo. To note a pathetic oversight in protocol, when the merchant ships were sunk, they were not even afforded the privilege of being classed as a "war grave," as their crews were not in the "armed forces."

The convoys would generally assemble on the west coast of Scotland, or off Iceland, prior to sailing for Murmansk, Polyarnoe, or Archangel. The escort would invariably have a heavy cruiser as the flagship to try to deter and protect against the ever-present threat of the *Tirpitz* hiding in the northern

Norwegian fjords. There would also be a number of destroyers to protect against the U-boats. These fast and agile ships were equipped with ASDIC (this equipment was developed by a specially established committee, the Anti Submarine Detection and Investigation Committee, hence the acronym ASDIC) to detect submarines and depth charges to sink them. They were very effective and much feared by the U-boat commanders.

The convoy would also have a number of minesweepers, corvettes, and armed trawlers in their escort. All the warships had anti-aircraft guns to guard against the most serious threat, which came from the air. The Luftwaffe had long-range reconnaissance aircraft, dive bombers, and torpedo bombers stationed at Kirkenes, Banuk, Tromsoe, and Narvik in northern Norway. These aircraft could attack a convoy for the last part of its journey all around the northern tip of Norway, and almost to Murmansk itself.

Paradoxically, the bad weather that made the seamen's lives such misery actually protected them. It made it difficult for U-boats to operate at periscope depth, and the cloud cover prevented the reconnaissance aircraft and bombers from operating effectively.

The perceived threat that the *Tirpitz* posed to the Arctic convoys was completely out of proportion to her importance, and represented a stunning victory for the Germans. As they began to realise the significance of the Arctic convoys, the German high command began to make plans to station major surface units in northern Norway. The Germans also planned to build up the number of U-boats patrolling the convoy routes, and increase the number of bombers and long-range reconnaissance aircraft in their newly acquired air bases in the region. Hitler was very reluctant to expose the *Tirpitz* to the risk of air attack, and Grand Admiral Doenitz found it very difficult to get Hitler's approval to move the *Tirpitz* from the Baltic.

The *Tirpitz* was a battleship, the sister ship to the *Bismark*. She carried eight 15-inch guns that each fired a projectile weighing 1,960 pounds. Churchill and the Admiralty were still in a state of shock following the sinking of their major battleship, the *Hood*, which had blown up and sunk immediately after a direct hit from one of the *Bismark*'s 15-inch guns. More than 1,500 men had been lost and only two survivors picked up. The Royal Navy subsequently hounded the *Bismark* to death and sunk her in the Atlantic. That loss had, in turn, left a lasting impression on Hitler who, unbeknown to Churchill, had subsequently banned his capital ships from any further sorties into the Atlantic. So concerned was the Royal Navy about the *Tirpitz* a plan was considered that would require two or three battleships of the King George V class to counter the threat that she posed. This was despite the fact that the King George V had 10 14-inch guns each firing a projectile weighing 1,590 pounds.

The Germans had another serious problem of which the British Admiralty was unaware; the *Tirpitz* used heavy fuel oil, and this was in extremely short supply compared with the diesel oil used by most of the other German ships.

In December 1941, Admiral Raeder met with Hitler to request permission to relocate the *Tirpitz* to northern Norway. Again Hitler refused, and it was not until January 12,1942, that he finally agreed. The *Tirpitz* moved on the night of the January 15, and anchored 15 miles east of Trondheim in Asafjiord. RAF reconnaissance aircraft located her there on January 23, heavily camouflaged and surrounded with anti-submarine nets. This confirmed Churchill's worst fears. He wrote at the time "the destruction or even crippling of this ship is the greatest event at sea at the present time. No other target is comparable to it. If she were even only crippled it would be difficult to take her back to Germany. The whole strategy of the war turns at this period on this ship, which is holding four times the number of British ships paralysed, to say nothing of the two new American battleships retained in the Atlantic."

The RAF mounted a bombing raid with 16 aircraft on the night of January 29, without success. In late February, Hitler authorised Admiral Raeder to reinforce the *Tirpitz* with the pocket battleship *Scheer*, mounted with formidable 11-inch guns, and the cruiser *Prinz Eugen*. As the British approached Trondheim, the submarine *Trident* managed to torpedo the *Prinz Eugen* and damage her enough that she would be out of action for eight months.

On March 1, the outbound convoy PQ12 sailed from Iceland; on the same day, the returning QP8 sailed from Murmansk. On March 5, a German reconnaissance aircraft sighted PQ12, and Hitler gave his approval for the *Tirpitz* to sail to intercept it. Fortunately, she was sighted by a patrolling submarine who reported her position to the Admiralty. On March 7, the two convoys passed each other and the *Tirpitz* failed to intercept them. She was heading back to base when aircraft from the carrier *Victorious* managed to locate her. The *Victorious* then launched 12 torpedo-carrying Albacore aircraft which proceeded to attack the *Tirpitz*. Somehow, she managed to avoid all the torpedoes, and even shot down two of the aircraft. This was to be best opportunity that the Royal Navy would have to attack the *Tirpitz* and, sadly, it failed. However, Admiral Ciliax on the *Tirpitz* was convinced that she had been hit by two torpedoes that had failed to explode. The attack badly worried Admiral Raeder, who asked Hitler to provide more air cover and to reinforce the northern fleet. For its part, the Admiralty was painfully aware that, not only had a perfect chance been missed to tip the balance of power in their favour, but also that PQ12 and QP8 had narrowly missed disaster. The threat still remained.

On March 19, the cruiser *Hipper*, with 8-inch guns, sailed north undetected to join the *Tirpitz* and the *Scheer* at Trondheim. The stakes were now being raised in the fight for supremacy on the Arctic convoy routes. At the end of March, the RAF mounted another raid on the *Tirpitz* with 33 bombers, but this also failed to significantly damage the ship. The RAF attacked again on the April 28 and 29; again, the attacks failed. The stakes were raised another notch in May when the pocket battleship *Lutzow* arrived to join her sister ship, the *Scheer*.

In June 1942, the large outbound convoy PQ17 was due to sail with 35 ships. The Germans were preparing a plan, known as operation "Knights Move" (Roesselsprung) to stop this convoy. Under this plan, the surface fleet was to be split into two groups. The Trondheim group, comprised of the *Tirpitz*, the *Hipper*, and six destroyers, would attack the convoy escort ships. The Narvik group, comprised of the *Lutzow* and the *Scheer*, also with six destroyers, would attack the merchant ships. When Admiral Raeder had presented the plan to Hitler in mid-June, he had received only guarded approval, conditional on the British aircraft carriers being located and put out of action. This would severely limit the Germans' freedom to operate.

PQ17 finally sailed on June 27, and was located by the Germans on July 1. Because of bad weather, it was not until July 3 that the RAF was able to confirm that the *Tirpitz* and the other capital ships had left their moorings. Its worst fears confirmed, panic gripped the Admiralty, and the stage seemed set for a major engagement. What was not known was the extent of the restrictions placed on his fleet by Hitler, the extent of the fuel shortage affecting the *Tirpitz*, and the fact that the *Lutzow* and three destroyers had run aground while leaving their moorings, and were out of action.

The First Sea Lord, Admiral Sir Dudley Pound, now faced the most difficult decision of his career. He knew that the cruisers escorting the convoy were no match for the *Tirpitz*, and that, without the cruiser escort, the massed ships of the convoy would be defenceless and easy prey. After much deliberation, Admiral Pound finally gave the order for the cruisers to retire west at high speed, and for the convoy to scatter. This fateful decision was to have disastrous effects. The *Tirpitz* was nowhere near the convoy. Due to all the restrictions placed on her, she was just off the North Cape. As soon as news reached her that the convoy had scattered, she headed back to her moorings, correctly assuming that the U-boats and the Luftwaffe could clean up; and clean up they did.

The next few days were a catalogue of hell, of suffering, and of heroism. The U-boats sank 10 ships. The Luftwaffe, deploying 200 aircraft, sank 14 ships for the loss of only six aircraft. Only 11 ships survived from the convoy. Of 157,000 tons of cargo, only 57,000 tons arrived. The losses included 430 tanks, 210 aircraft, and 3,350 trucks. It was an unmitigated disaster, with hundreds of lives lost, all for the threat of one ship that never actually fired a shot in the action. The Soviet reaction was typically unsympathetic. They simply said that the convoys should be bigger and better protected.

By September, the RAF had torpedo aircraft in Murmansk. Hitler, fearing for the safety of his capital ships, had already contacted Admiral Raeder and warned him not to risk them unless he was completely sure of results. Raeder had already moved the *Tirpitz* and other capital ships to Altenfjord on the North Cape to be closer to the convoy routes.

Churchill now decided to advance a novel plan to attack the *Tirpitz*, as all attempts at bombing her had failed. This plan was to use newly developed miniature submarines, called X-craft. The first of these was launched in May of 1943 and a rushed program was underway to mount an attack on September 22, when the tidal conditions would be favourable.

The X-craft was a true miniature submarine; 50 feet long and 5 1/2 feet in diameter at the widest point. It carried a crew of two officers and two ratings, one of whom was a diver. The diver was equipped with an oxygen rebreathing set so as not to leave any tell tale bubbles, and special cutting equipment to allow him to free the submarine should it become trapped in anti-submarine nets. One person could stand in the conning tower, the rest of the crew were permanently and uncomfortably doubled up. The X-craft had a diesel engine that powered it at 6 knots on the surface and batteries that enabled it to maintain 4 knots submerged. The X-craft had limited range, both in fuel and crew endurance. In view of this limit, they were to be towed to Norway behind conventional submarines. These were the *Thrasher* towing X5, the *Truculent* towing X6, the *Stubborn* towing X7, the *Seanymph* towing X8, the *Syrtis* towing X9, and the *Sceptre* towing X10.

The *Tirpitz* was moored in a small fjord called Kaafjord which lies at the head of Altenfjord. She was to be attacked by X5, X6, and X7. The battle cruiser *Scharnhorst* was also in

Altenfjiord, and she moored in the shelter of a small island called Aaroy. She was to be attacked by X9 and X10. The X8 was to attack the *Lutzow*.

Each X-craft was fitted with two, 2-ton explosive charges that could be dropped independently and set with a delay time fuse. The six X-craft left the west of Scotland under tow on the night of September 11. On the night of the 15th, the tow line to X8 broke, and she was on her own until she managed to find the *Stubborn* towing X7. She then developed mechanical problems and had to be scuttled. Early the next morning the *Syrtis* found that her tow had broken and she had lost X9. Despite a detailed search, X9 and her crew were never seen again. The remaining four X-craft were safely delivered to their rendezvous on the Norwegian coast where the crews were changed for the operational crews that were to make the attack. They left their mother submarines on September 20. X7 was nearly lost when her mine tangled up on her bow. Her Captain, Lieutenant Place, managed to kick it free and, accompanied by Lieutenant Henty Henty-Creer in X5, Lieutenant Cameron in X6, and Lieutenant Hudspeth in X10, they set off up the fjord. On the way, X10 broke down and had to drop out of the action. The other three hid during the day among some small islands near the entrance to Kaafjiord and in the early hours of the 22nd moved in for attack. X7 went first and became tangled in the anti-submarine nets. It took

them more than an hour to extricate themselves. X6 managed to get in by following a motorboat through an opening in the nets. She then ran aground and broke surface while trying to free herself. She was seen by the Germans, but they were remarkably slow to react. She was able to drop both her charges under the forward turret of the *Tirpitz*. Realising that escape was impossible, Lieutenant Cameron scuttled the X6 and the crew were picked up by a German motorboat.

Having freed herself, the X7 now managed to lay both her charges under the keel of the *Tirpitz* and tried to make good her escape. She got caught in the nets again and on freeing herself sustained damage that prevented her from staying submerged. The Germans opened fire on her and Lieutenant Place managed to scramble onto a buoy before she sank with the rest of her crew. To his surprise, he was joined two hours later by his crewman, sub Lieutenant Aitken, who had managed to escape from the wreck before his air ran out.

The captain of the *Tirpitz* tried to raise steam to get away, but was too late. He reduced the damage by moving the ship as much as he could on its moorings. The four charges went off simultaneously, with the eight tons of explosives lifting the *Tirpitz* bodily by several feet. Although still afloat, she was mortally wounded and would never sail again. She was finally sent to the bottom by the RAF some months later. Lieutenants Place and Cameron were both awarded the Victoria Cross and, along with the other survivors, spent the rest of the war in a German prison camp.

The X5 with Henty Henty-Creer and his crew were never seen again. The Germans claimed to have sunk an X-craft just outside the nets. It was not known whether or not he had pressed home the attack, but he received no posthumous award.

The crippling of the *Tirpitz* marked the turning of the tide in the battle for control of the Arctic routes, and removed a dreadful threat that had so affected the Admiraly's every move. It is hard to believe that one ship could do so much damage by the very possibility of its presence, without even firing a shot in anger.

By an amazing coincidence in 1974, I sponsored a diving expedition to Kaafjiord to locate the wreck of X5, and try to determine whether Henty Henty-Creer had pressed home the attack. We did find the wreck of X5 close to where the *Tirpitz* had been moored, but even with that information, no posthumous award was forthcoming for Henty Henty-Creer. My souvenir of that adventure is a large white coffee pot from the *Tirpitz* stamped with the German double-headed eagle.

To put the action of the German surface fleet into context, they only sank three of the total of 100 ships lost on the Arctic convoys between 1941 and 1945. All those were in 1942, which was by far the blackest year for the convoys, with a total of 63 ships lost. Over the entire five-year period, the U-boats accounted for 42 losses and aircraft for 38. The remaining 17 were sunk by mines and weather. 1942 stands out starkly as the year the tide turned. Only one ship was lost in 1941 and only four in 1943.

Over the span of the convoys from 1941 to 1945, Britain and America shipped to the Soviet Union more than 12,000 tanks, 20,000 aircraft, 12,000 anti-aircraft guns, 400,000 assorted motor vehicles, 500,000,000 rounds of various sizes of ammunition, 350,000 tons of explosives, 135,000 rifles, and millions of tons of fuel and other supplies. It is hardly surprising that the Soviet Union retained such military might long after the end of the war.

The 5 1/2 tons of gold shipped in the *Edinburgh* was valued at the time at £1,500,000 and represented payment for only 0.5% of the total value of goods shipped by Great Britain.

To help protect against the threat from the Luftwaffe, a number of the merchant vessels called CAM ships (Catapult Aircraft Merchant) were equipped with catapult-launched Hurricane fighters. The pilots of these aircraft were incredibly brave men.

They would be launched to engage attacking bombers, and then had only two options, both equally unpalatable; they could ditch the fighter in the sea alongside a convoy vessel and pray that they were picked up before they died from exposure, or fly east and try to find somewhere to land in northern Russia. This latter option entailed the danger of running out of fuel and ditching at sea away from the convoy with little prospect of survival, as well as the danger of not finding a suitable landing place in Russia. Even if they did find a place to land, they were plagued by the uncertainty of how and when they would get home.

On the outbound convoy PQ16 in May 1942, the Germans launched an attack with torpedo bombers. The CAM ship Empire Lawrence launched its Hurricane piloted by Flight Lieutenant Hay. Hay succeeded in shooting down two of the attacking aircraft and driving the rest away, thus preventing any damage to the convoy. As he flew back to the convoy at low level to ditch and be picked up, other ships in the convoy mistook him for a German and shot him down. Hay was badly wounded, but was rapidly rescued by the destroyer Volunteer and became one of the lucky CAM pilots to live to tell the tale.

With these options before them it is a miracle that they ever launched, but launch they did and their presence deterred the Luftwaffe bombers and successfully broke up attack formations. The Hurricane was universally feared and the German bombers had little fighter cover. These brave pilots undoubtedly saved many convoy ships and countless lives.

The cruisers, such as the Edinburgh, carried much slower Walrus float planes. These were catapult-launched and could land on the sea alongside their mother ship and be recovered by crane, provided, of course, the sea was calm enough.

On the outbound convoys, the Germans would concentrate their attacks on the merchant vessels to prevent their cargoes from reaching the Russian front. On the way back the empty merchant vessels were of too little value to justify the expenditure of valuable munitions on their destruction, so the undivided attention of the Germans was focused on the warship escorts.

PQ14 left Scotland outbound on April 8, 1942. The voyage to Murmansk had passed with only the loss of one merchant vessel off Bear Island; heavy cloud cover had kept the Luftwaffe grounded at their northern bases for most of the time. At Murmansk, the crew stayed on board the Edinburgh while the merchant ships of the convoy were unloaded and prepared for the return journey. Murmansk was virtually under siege and was being regularly bombed. There was no entertainment on shore, and, despite the help that they were receiving from Britain, the Russians were suspicious, not helpful, and frequently downright obstructive.

Shortly before sailing, a Russian steam tug was brought alongside the *Edinburgh*. A call was put out for seamen who spoke French and a working party was assembled to unload 93 wooden boxes from the tug. The Russian officers did not speak English, but several of them spoke French. The *Edinburgh's* work party was under the command of Commander Jefferies.

With a layer of fresh snow on the deck, it was bitterly cold. The 93 wooden boxes were craned aboard from the tug and stacked on the deck of the *Edinburgh*. The boxes were of roughly sawn wood with rope handles at either end. Each one had a thin wire binding sealed on the top with two circular lead seals. Each box had Cyrillic inscriptions stencilled in red on the woodwork.

The boxes were slung two at a time in a rope sling with a pulley block and lowered by hand down a shaft in the centre of the vessel to the bomb room. This room was approximately 15 feet by 15 feet square, located deep below the waterline, and used to store the bombs for the Walrus aircraft. The bottom of the shaft gave access to a corridor on the centre line of the ship. From this corridor, a door led to starboard

into the bomb room, with a door opposite to port leading into an identical room used for storing munitions and fuses. Part of the work detail was stationed at the bottom of the shaft to unsling the boxes and carry them into the bomb room.

The working party had no idea what the boxes contained; to them it was just another job in the daily routine of running a large warship. Suddenly there was a crash and a shout. One of the boxes had slipped out of the rope sling and crashed to the floor of the shaft, narrowly missing the men working below. There was a stunned silence. The box had broken open and lying in its wreckage, surrounded by the sawdust that they were packed in, were four large, gleaming gold bars!

Commander Jefferies arrived on the double. The ship's carpenter was called to repair and repack the broken case. He and the working party were sworn to secrecy and read the Official Secrets Act. Despite all these efforts, it was impossible to keep a secret in the tight-knit community of a warship at sea and word spread through the ship like wildfire.

Back on deck, where he had returned to supervise the loading the remainder of the gold, Commander Jefferies met immediate trouble from the crew. The boxes were stacked on deck waiting to be lowered to the bomb room.

The damaged stern of the HMS Edinburgh. *(Photo courtesy of the Imperial War Museum)*

Heat from galley vents below deck melted the snow beneath the boxes and, in the process, dissolved some of the red stencilling on the cases. The reddened slush was running away into the scuppers. One of the working party said to Commander Jefferies, "I don't like it, sir, all this Russian gold running with blood, it's a bad omen."

As word spread through the ship, the crew was quick to realise that if the Germans knew of this shipment they would be even more of a prime target on the return journey than the flagship normally would have been.

Little did they know how right their premonitions would be.

THE SEARCH

FOR THE *EDINBURGH*

CHAPTER 5

I listened patiently to Keith recounting the bare facts of this story and of the subsequent sinking. Hundreds of questions sprang to mind, but at that time Keith knew little more than the basic facts gleaned from the Public Records Office. This was where, critically, he had found a copy of the reccipt signed by Captain Faulkner for the 5 1/2 tons of gold loaded aboard the *Edinburgh* on that freezing day in Murmansk.

Was the gold really loaded? There were so many *ruse de guerre* and deceptions at the time that we would need hard evidence that the gold was really there before going any further.

How did we know that no one had taken some, or all, of the gold off before the vessel sank?

How accurate was the information on the site of the sinking?

opp. page: The Stephaniturm *at sea.*
(Photo by J. Clarke)

What was the actual depth of the vessel? Could we locate the wreck? Could we realistically dive on her with our existing technology?

Was the gold still in the bomb room, or had it been moved or lost by the torpedo damage; or, had the impact of the wreck hitting the seabed scattered it throughout the ship?

Had anyone else been there before us and pirated the cargo from the wreck?

Who now owned the bullion, and could we negotiate a watertight and legally binding contract with the owners to protect our position?

Keith Jessop was, at the time, a shallow-water diver who had worked for us offshore on several occasions, but he did not have a diving company of his own, nor any equipment or finance. He was basically looking for someone to take the risk and fund a salvage attempt with him getting a percentage of the proceeds for his information, but not actually risking any of his own money. Keith's input to earn his share had to be having the idea in the first place, and carrying out all the research work. Keith is an ebullient man and an eternal optimist. It is to his undying credit that he never once flagged in his enthusiasm and unshakeable conviction that we would back him, and that we would find and salvage the gold.

I slowly drew out the answers to my questions and began to build up a credible picture of problems that would face us if we took on the project. Not only was there Captain Faulkner's receipt for the gold being loaded on board, but also an exchange of signals with the Admiralty after the *Edinburgh* was abandoned.

With rather tactless haste in such tragic circumstances, the Admiralty signalled Bonham-Carter to ask if he had managed to save the gold. His terse reply stated simply that "the gold was in a compartment that was flooded by the first torpedo."

More prosaic evidence of the gold's existence came from the matter of correspondence covering the insurance claim for the loss of the gold. It transpired that the bullion had been insured in thirds; one third by Lloyds, and two thirds by the Black Sea and Baltic Insurance Company in London. The Black Sea and Baltic was a subsidiary of Ingostrakh, the Soviet state insurance company. The claim was paid out for the value at the time of some £1.5 million. Lloyds was reimbursed under the Government War Risks arrangements.

This left the Soviet government owning two thirds of the bullion and the British government owning the other third. These percentages were to be of great significance when the salvage proceeds were divided up.

With good evidence of the existence of the gold in my hands, I cross-examined Keith in detail concerning the location of the wreck. Kapitan Max Teichert in U-456 had recorded the position where his torpedoes had first struck the *Edinburgh*, but the Germans used a different navigation system than the Royal Navy, and the *Edinburgh* had manoeuvred erratically for some 48 hours after that fix.

The *Edinburgh* herself had recorded the position, but that too was very unreliable. Back then, the navigators used a system of "dead reckoning" — recording course, speed, and time from the last known fix until they could get another accurate astronomical fix using a sextant. Heavy overcast conditions and fog had prevented her from getting a good fix, and her dead reckoning would have been hopelessly inaccurate with all the course and speed changes she made before finally dropping below the surface.

A number of other escorts provided positions, including the Russian destroyers and British minesweepers that were called out from Murmansk to pick up survivors.

In addition, there were more modern positions given by Norwegian fishing vessels in the sixties and seventies that had snagged a wreck in the vicinity. One of these had actually dredged up a depth charge launcher that was positively identified as coming from the *Edinburgh*. These positions were based on the Decca survey system that had considerable errors in northern latitudes.

We had a wealth of information, but the positions covered an area 60 miles by 60 miles: the size of greater London. To make matters worse, the water depth in this area varied from 800 feet to 1,500 feet. By now I was extremely nervous because I knew that we could not contemplate a manned dive of more than 1,000 feet.

I still required a great deal more evidence as to whether or not the gold would still be in the bomb room. That was to prove excruciatingly difficult to obtain.

My other major worry was whether anyone had been there before us. Little was then known of the Soviet diving capabilities, but we had to assume that they would be technically competent, and they most certainly knew that the gold was there.

Before the development of commercial diving, some very impressive salvage operations had been carried out using a technique known as "blast and grab." The salvors would drag a wire across the seabed fixed between two ships until they snagged a wreck. They would then lower a man in an atmospheric observation chamber. This was a tube with windows that a man was bolted into and remained at atmospheric pressure.

It was equipped with lights and a telephone. The operator would direct the ship to move around on its anchors until the chamber was in the right position. He would then direct the ship to lower explosives onto the wreck to open it up. After the explosives had been fired he would go down again and direct a grab lowered from the salvage vessel to drag away the wreckage.

Eventually, by patient and laborious work they would expose the cargo which would be salvaged. Then, by following the same process they would recover the cargo. This form of salvage was immensely time consuming and very weather dependant (not to mention destructive). Yet profitable salvages were possible in the early part of this century when time and labour were cheap.

World War I left an enormous number of wrecks on the seabed loaded with non-ferrous metals such as copper, tin, lead, and zinc. World War II added even further to this stockpile of wealth just waiting to be salvaged.

In January 1917, the 15,000-ton White Star liner *Laurentic* struck a mine off Lough Swilly, Northern Ireland. In her second class baggage room were 3,211 gold ingots valued at £5 million. The wreck lay in 135 feet of water. Between 1917 and 1924, 3,186 ingots were recovered using air divers in an heroic effort of old-style salvage.

The "blast and grab" method was perfected by an Italian company called Sorima, led by the rotund and ebullient Captain Quaglia who was a larger-than-life salvor to the core. In 1930 they made history by salvaging £ 1 million of gold bullion from the *Egypt* in 400 feet of water 30 miles off the coast of Brittany with their salvage vessel the *Artiglio.*

Until the *Edinburgh* salvage, the *Egypt* salvage was the world record holder for water depth, and the *Laurentic* for value. After that success, Sorima was contracted by the French government to clear a World War I wreck, loaded with ammunition, near Quiberon off Brittany. This was quite an easy job for Quaglia after the *Egypt*. It was the usual tedious and drawn out blast and grab operation with the salvage vessel moving away a safe distance each time an underwater charge was fired. As the job dragged on they became complacent, until one day, not having moved off far enough, they were caught in a massive explosion of the ordinance in the wreck set off by one of their own demolition charges. The results were catastrophic: the *Artiglio* was blown to pieces and sunk, killing three of their best divers and most of the crew.

In later years, their mantle was assumed by the enormously successful British firm, Risdon Beazley. They refined the blast and grab operation to the "state of the art." Risdon Beazley formed close links with the Salvage Association, a non-profit organisation funded by insurance underwriters and ship owners' organisations specifically to arrange the salvage of abandoned cargos, the ownership of which had reverted to the underwriters.

Risdon employed a full-time researcher and, based on his work, approached the Salvage Association for contracts on their target wrecks. The contracts were always "no cure, no pay" where the salvor paid all the costs and took all the risk and the Salvage Association (on behalf of the legal owner of the cargo) received a percentage of the value of cargo recovered. In the case of non-ferrous metals, this was usually a low figure, in the order of 20%, as the upside for the salvor was not that great.

In the fifties and sixties Risdon Beazley prospered. They had no real competition in waters deeper than the limits of air diving, and the oil industry had not yet spawned a deep-diving industry. They were tenacious in the extreme. On one occasion they were awarded a contract to recover a small quantity of gold bullion from the wreck of a vessel called the *Empire Manor*, lost off the east coast of Canada.

When she sank, the *Empire Manor* had nose dived into the seabed. When they blew into the bullion room they found that the weight of gold had burst through the forward bulkhead and the cupboard was bare. Undeterred, they worked their way along the wreck following the path of the gold and finally caught up with it at the very bow of the wreck in the anchor chain locker.

This story was burnt into my memory and was to cause us much heartache in the planning of the *Edinburgh* salvage.

While having a good professional reputation, Risdon Beazley were not completely respected by others in the diving community. There were persistent rumours (probably from jealous competitors) that they had helped themselves to a number of cargos without the burden of a contract. While this would be hard to prove, the rumours were enough to cause me to grill Keith Jessop at length concerning the risk that Risdon Beazley had already quietly removed the gold. Keith was unable to completely suppress my doubts, but felt that they could not have got away with such a large amount of gold without the story leaking out. Also, Keith informed me that Risdon Beazley were sniffing around and had already spoken to the Salvage Association about the *Edinburgh*.

By this stage of the conversation on that Saturday afternoon, while Malcolm was digging his garden, my enthusiasm was well aroused. Provided that all the information was correct, our company 2W could certainly do the work. The talk now turned to the sixty-four thousand dollar question of whether or not we could get a watertight contract with the two governments to secure our title to the wreck, and protect the vast investment that would be required.

During the previous year, Keith had worked for a Norwegian diving company called Seaway, and had persuaded them to take a survey vessel up to the area to try to locate the wreck. This had been a miserable failure and the parties had fallen out.

Keith had by this time realised that, if he was to progress with the project, he would need to set up his own company and get some professional help. He established Jessop Marine Recoveries Limited (JMRL) as his vehicle for the project. Unfortunately, Keith's judgment of people left much to be desired. He brought in a former naval officer named James Ringrose, whose only claim to fame seemed to be that he had once served on the same ship as Prince Charles. While he professed to be a diving expert, Malcolm and I had never heard of him and it soon became clear that he had only superficial knowledge of commercial diving and it was unlikely that he could have held down a job in the diving industry. Malcolm and I refused to deal with him and later, Keith was to suffer greatly at the hands of his partners.

The other addition to Keith's stable was a small hatchet-faced lawyer called David Bona. He was undoubtedly a clever man, perhaps too clever. We found Mr. Bona to be pedantic and verbose to the point of ridicule and he single-handedly did vast damage to the timber reserves of the Amazon Basin by his consumption of paper. It was the standing joke in our office that he must have been getting paid by the line.

When the meeting finally broke up on that Saturday, I had committed 2W to the project on the basis that we would fund and execute the project and receive 90% of the proceeds. JMRL would receive 10% in recognition of their research and original idea to pursue the project.

There followed several months of prolonged negotiation and obfuscation with Mr. Bona. It soon became clear that Malcolm and I had a vast amount of work to do in planning and preparation, so Keith was left with the responsibility to lead the negotiations with the Salvage Association and the principals accompanied by us.

Malcolm and I started the planning. It was clear that the operation had to fall into two separate phases. First, we had to locate and identify the wreck and film it. At that stage, it might prove to be too deep, or the wreck may have been pillaged already, or the access to the bomb room may prove too difficult. If we succeeded in finding the wreck, we considered that there was a 50% chance that we would have to abort at that stage. We rated the overall chance of a successful recovery at about 10-20%.

We estimated that the total cost of the salvage operation would be in the order of £3 million pounds, with the survey operation costing about £500,000 of that. Malcolm and I were not rich. We had sunk all our available savings into starting up 2W and, although the company was doing well, our profits were being channelled into expansion and the acquisition of new equipment. We were fighting hard to build our market share in an industry where the oil companies still regarded newcomers with suspicion; in their eyes we were still earning our technical spurs.

The trick for us would be to assemble a consortium of partners who we trusted. They would come to the party "no cure no pay" and so would bear their share of the downside if we failed, and their share in the upside if we succeeded. Our first priority was the survey phase. We would need a survey vessel (which was the largest cost element), competent surveyors, and a Remotely Operated Vehicle (ROV) capable of operating down to 450 metres (1,500 feet), the maximum depth in the search area.

It had always been my basic tenet of the diving business to never own the support vessels. They are profitable when working, but really drain you when they are idle. Their ownership should be the responsibility of a professional ship owner. We had been working for some time with a German shipping company, the Offshore Supply Association of Bremen (OSA) and particularly knew John Clarke, who was a senior project manager with them. They had a small diving ship called *Stephaniturm* that had a good saturation diving system and a dynamic positioning system to keep the vessel on station without anchors, as it would be virtually impossible to anchor a ship in the depths we were expecting.

OSA also had a smaller vessel suitable for the survey work. After some discussion, they agreed in principal to join the consortium for 50.4% of the salvor's income (they were to have the largest financial risk). OSA gave John Clarke the overall responsibility for the project, with considerable freedom of action and direct access to senior management. This decision greatly enhanced the efficiency of the project.

We next turned to the surveyors. John Clarke, who himself was a former naval hydrographic surveyor, knew Kip Punch of Rascal Decca. Rascal Decca stood out as a very professional and well-equipped company with the most modern survey equipment. They came on board, no cure no pay, for 2.48% of the salvor's income.

Malcolm and I had all the divers and diving technology and, most importantly, a

state-of-the-art ROV, the "Scorpio," that we had just bought for a million dollars from its US manufacturer.

All the preparations went ahead at a furious pace, but we still did not have an actual contract for the salvage. Nevertheless, we pushed on in the blind faith of Keith's eternal optimism that we would get the contract. All this was going on at the height of the cold war and the Salvage Association, while having carte blanche to negotiate on behalf of the British government, were finding the Soviets very difficult to deal with. We had assumed that our consortium was the only player in the running for the contract, and were concerned to find that Seaway had requested to bid and had also tried to make contact with the Soviets in Moscow. To make matters worse, Risdon Beazley had reared their head and asked the Salvage Association if they could bid as well.

While Keith was furious about this latest development, I took great comfort from it. It meant to me that it was very unlikely that Risdon Beazley had previously pirated the wreck, and that fact removed one of my main nagging worries.

Keith was now in a black mood; he had thought that the project would be ours on favourable terms and now his pet project was being seriously threatened. An emergency meeting was called in my office to discuss tactics. I took over the meeting as I was on familiar ground, deciding what price to bid for a competitive tender. I reviewed what information we had.

Keith knew from his time with Seaway that they considered 50% for the salvor to be a good deal. They might well go below that in a sealed bid. On the other hand, they were Norwegian and this was very much a British operation on a British warship. The Ministry of Defence (MoD) would not be able to exert so much pressure on a Norwegian firm.

Furthermore, I knew that they had upset the Salvage Association by going over their heads and dealing directly to the Soviets. However, both they and Keith Jessop had written permission from the Salvage Association to film, but not touch the wreck. Seaway could rely on that to go back and look again. Rumours abounded that they were preparing for a second survey trip.

Risdon Beazley was definitely a more complex problem. I knew they had very close personal relationships with the Salvage Association going back over many years, and would not hesitate to work that angle. They usually worked on very high salvor's percentages of about 80% for non-ferrous metals, and would probably baulk at going down to 50%. In the mid-fifties, Risdon Beazley had contacted the MoD

about the *Edinburgh* and had been given permission to attempt a salvage operation. After very careful consideration they had calculated the risks too great and decided not to proceed.

Paradoxically, it was only two or three years later that another branch of the MoD classified the *Edinburgh* as a war grave. Our greatest advantage was that Risdon Beazley still only had blast and grab technology, and would have to blow the wreck apart to get at the gold. I could not see the MoD or public opinion allowing them to cause so much disturbance to the wreck. I did not, however, underestimate Risdon's ability to put pressure on their long-standing contacts in the Salvage Association. We had heard rumours that they were planning an Arctic expedition, and had to assume that they too were going to try to find her, and could possibly rely on their permission from the fifties as a legal fig leaf to cover their present activities.

By then, we had already made a detailed presentation to the Salvage Association and representatives of the MoD on how a diving salvage operation would be conducted. Access would depend on how the wreck was lying, but would be achieved by burning a hole through the hull approximately 10 feet by 10 feet square. Further holes of a similar size would be burnt in any internal bulkheads we had to remove to get to the bomb room. By working in this way, it would not be necessary to disturb any other parts of the wreck. I felt this meeting had gone well and that the MoD, in particular, was on our side. I also felt strongly that there would be great reluctance to award the contract to a foreign company.

There followed a heated discussion about tactics for bidding. Keith felt we should not go below 50% for the salvor's share. I said that we were looking at a known cargo of 5 1/2 tons of gold worth nearly £50 million. If we found any of it we were likely to find all or most of it. I recall that my actual words were, "It's a fortune anyway, let's stop screwing around and go in at 45 percent." This was precisely the way that we would handle a big lump sum offshore diving bid. Everyone agreed, and on that basis our bid proved successful.

After we submitted the bid, there was an agonising period of waiting while the Salvage Association sought Soviet approval. While we could have started the survey phase based on Keith's previous approval, both Malcolm and I had learned "not to put our trust in princes" and wanted both parties fully committed. To finally get this commitment, Keith, accompanied and much assisted by the OSA project manager, John Clarke, accompanied a British government team and the Salvage Association on a presentation trip to Moscow.

By then we knew that the contract was almost ours, and set about our preparations with renewed vigour. We would not actually sail until the Soviet approval came, which was enormously frustrating. It also made it difficult for OSA to schedule availability of the survey vessel that was to be the *Dammtor*.

Led by Kip Punch, another formal naval officer and an expert surveyor, the Racal Decca part of the team swung into action. Punch worked very closely with John Clarke who, as a surveyor himself, was heavily involved in the detailed analysis of every piece of positional information we had. They analysed the information's likely accuracy and possible error. Having ascribed a probability of accuracy to each position, they concluded that the most accurate fixes were those of the minesweepers based at Murmansk that had come out to pick up survivors, and had arrived just before the sinking. These ships had been the least time at sea, and had made the least course changes so their dead reckoning positions should be the most accurate. Of these, Kip selected HMS *Harrier* as the most reliable position and it was agreed that we should search that area first.

Having chosen our first target, we could now consider the implications of that information. It showed an area which was technically in Norwegian water, but had long since claimed by the Soviet Union. This area was therefore blighted

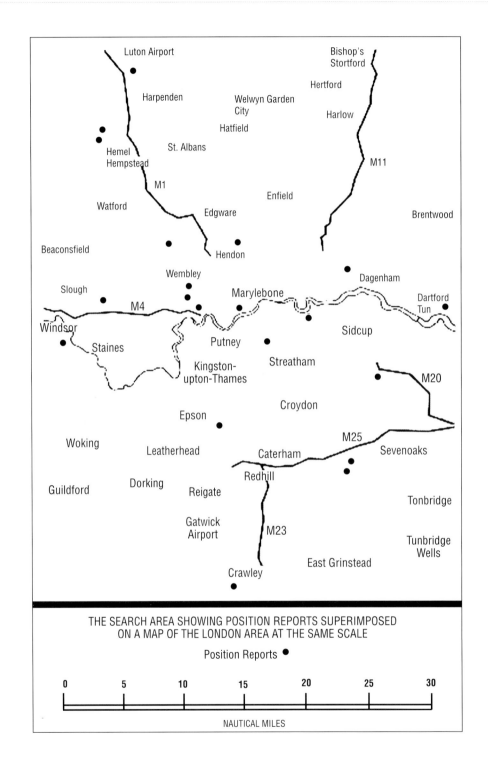

THE SEARCH AREA SHOWING POSITION REPORTS SUPERIMPOSED
ON A MAP OF THE LONDON AREA AT THE SAME SCALE

Position Reports ●

0   5   10   15   20   25   30

NAUTICAL MILES

The side scan sonar on the Dammtor *that found the wreck of HMS* Edinburgh. *(Photo by J. Clarke)*

for fishing and oil exploration and had become known as the "grey zone." With the endless prevarication from the Soviets, we had contemplated sailing to start the survey without waiting for their formal approval. With the primary search area now directed at the grey zone, this was out of the question. The Soviets considered it their waters and patrolled it regularly. Our survey vessel would stand out lie a sore thumb.

We had equipped the *Dammtor* with the latest side-scan sonar equipment. This unit is towed behind the survey vessel and emits sonar signals on both sides of its path. Like an underwater radar, these signals reflect back from objects on the seabed and are recorded on a paper chart. A wreck will show up as dark shadowed area on the chart. The plan was for any indications from the side scan sonar to be investigated by the "Scorpio" ROV.

The next problem to be considered was that of identification. The job of the survey team was to positively identify the wreck as the *Edinburgh* and to provide as much video footage as possible in order to confirm the condition of the wreck, how she was lying, and what would be the best route to the bomb room. If Kip Punch's hunch was correct as to *Edinburgh's* final resting place, then we knew that there was the wreck of the *Hermann Shoemann* lying nearby. Affectionately known to us as *Hermann Shoemann the German*, she was the destroyer sunk by *Edinburgh's* gunfire in her last engagement. Her silhouette was substantially different than that of the *Edinburgh*, but we would only be able to check that with an ROV survey which would be both costly and time-consuming.

The fact that the wreck of another and very similar heavy cruiser, the HMS *Trinidad*, was also believed to be in that area, was even more worrisome. The *Trinidad* had escorted the previous outbound convoy PQ13. They had come under attack by U-boats and by a German surface fleet. *Trinidad* had steamed into the attack engaging the enemy with her main turrets and had succeeded in sinking the destroyer Z 26. At the same time, she fired torpedoes at them. By an appalling stroke of bad luck, one of her shells fell short and exploded in the water in front of one of her torpedoes. The torpedo turned 180 degrees and headed back toward the *Trinidad*, where it caused massive damage and serious loss of life. The crew did a heroic job of damage control and, against all odds, managed to get the vessel to Murmansk, where she was put into the only available drydock.

The Russians did not have enough of the correct grade of steel plate to mend her so this was shipped out on the *Edinburgh* with PQ14. After the loss of the *Edinburgh*, her survivors waited until repairs on the Trinidad were completed and set sail for the UK on her together with Captain Faulkner and Admiral Bonham-Carter.

Sadly the Germans were waiting for her. They had been monitoring her progress on aerial reconnaissance photos and were determined to finish her off. They were helped by clear skies and bombed her incessantly for 24 hours. Finally, they managed to straddle her bridge with a stick of bombs, two of which penetrated deep into the ship and caused heavy loss of life and substantial fires. After the damage control officer reported to the bridge that it would take the entire Glasgow fire brigade to put out the fires, Bonham-Carter ordered the evacuation of his second cruiser. (The account of the loss of the *Trinidad* is recorded in a book called <u>The Ship That Torpedoed Itself</u>.)

Sadly a number of the *Edinburgh* survivors were lost on the *Trinidad* and the remainder, together with Faulkner and Bonham-Carter found their way back to Britain on smaller escorts and armed trawlers. This was after lengthy and very uncomfortable delays in Murmansk. A number more were tragically lost in the debacle of the homeward bound convoy QP13 in July 1942.

Unlike *Hermann Shoemann the German*, the *Trinidad* was a ship very similar to the *Edinburgh*. We had to carry out detailed research to identify the visual differences between the two. We were substantially aided by *Edinburgh's* sister ship, the *Belfast*. Moored as she is as a permanent museum on the River Thames in London in the pool upstream of Tower Bridge, we had easy access for our studies and were afforded great cooperation by her engine officer, who had sailed with John Clarke during his time in the Royal Navy. It became apparent that the principal identifying features were lattice-work steel stanchions that rose from main deck level to support decking above the torpedo launching tubes, the position of the torpedo launching tubes themselves, and the position of the ship's boats.

While all this was going on, the "Weasel" or "Bonehead" as David Bona was "affectionately" known in our office, had gone into overdrive and our telex machine almost overheated as it received reams of his pompous verbosity. Our own

The Belfast *moored at Tower Bridge. (Photo courtesy of the Imperial War Museum)*

lawyer, Nick Sinclair-Brown, was muttering darkly about unprofessionalism and single-handed conversion of a virgin rain forest into reams of telex paper.

The brutal truth of the matter was that Keith Jessop's role in the salvage was now at an end. He had provided the original idea, the necessary research and, with our backing, the contract. The rest of the job should now have been left to the professionals. It was at this stage of the project that Keith's greatest assets of self confidence and tenacity were to become his downfall. I can well understand that Keith would have an inferiority complex in dealing with us. We were successful entrepreneurs at the sharp end of an exciting new industry. Keith had no funds and lived in a council house in Keithly in Yorkshire. To his credit, whenever he did have money he spent it on research and the pursuit of his dream. His problem has always been a desire for publicity.

To put it into perspective, these are minor flaws of character found in most of us. Unfortunately, in these unique circumstances, they were to become a real problem for him. Keith had not had the benefit of exposure to the disciplines of a commercial existence and his fledgling £100 company Jessop Marine Services (JMRL) did not even have an office or a telephone. Bona ran it from the office of his law firm and was thereby able to exert much influence over Keith. Indeed, this lack of substance was a major stumbling block in getting the contract and, in the end, it was 2W's substance that, together with that of OSA and Decca, reassured both governments and was responsible for landing the contract.

Keith, aided by the missionary zeal of Bona, was now fighting a rear-guard action to keep as involved as possible.

During the original contract discussions between 2W and Keith, we had spent a lot of time discussing the Intellectual Property Rights (rights to publicity, etc.). This obviously meant a great deal to Keith, who wanted to see his name in lights. Malcolm and I were the mugs who were to risk the money and wanted the publicity rights as a fall-back if the salvage failed. We agreed that if we recovered less than £2 million pounds from the *Edinburgh*, 2W would keep all the publicity rights. If we found more than that, Keith would have 80% of the publicity rights, with 2W having 20%. As it turned out, this was to prove a personal disaster for Keith.

With the true blind faith of a prophet in his own time Keith, assuming that we would find all the gold, set out on the publicity trail, flirting with Yorkshire Television and the Daily Express. From the point of view of 2W and as the chief promoter of our company, I was keen on the right kind of publicity to help us to increase the sales of our Oilfield Diving services. At Comex we had seen the worst face of the press "ambulance chasing" and over-dramatising stories of diving accidents first-hand. We had seen reporters buying stories from divers in pubs and, on more than one occasion, had them threaten to make up stories about us if we did not give them information.

These experiences had left a lasting impression on Malcolm and me. For us, journalists were listed very low in the scale of life forms. We were working in a technically complex industry and had gotten to the forefront of that technology through hard work and a respected reputation. 2W had been established for four years by then and we had a clean record with no bad accidents. It was primordial to us to keep that record, and we would not accept having journalist poking into the running of our business.

At about this time, we faced another interesting problem. We had formed a partnership with a large American offshore group called Brown and Root (affectionately known in the business as "Root and Scoot"). They owned large construction barges for pipe lay and platform installation work. The joint venture with them gave us access to some major contracts that helped us build the company quickly. We were morally bound to run any diving contracts through them. Once we had enough details of the *Edinburgh* project, Malcolm telexed the president of Brown and Root, Hugh Gordon, laying out the risks and rewards of the operation, and asking if they wanted us to put it through the joint venture. Hugh Gordon was a larger-than-life Texan from an old Houston family. He was a bluff, honest, and immensely likable man, not dissimilar to Stormin' Norman of Gulf War fame. He was a

real entrepreneur who was extremely involved in the day-to-day operations of Brown and Root. Sadly, he was the last of his breed in an organization that has succumbed to bureaucracy.

Hugh duly telexed back to the effect that their board had determined that they were not in the treasure hunting business, and, if we wanted to proceed, we should do so with our own company. The framed original of that telex hung on Malcolm's office wall for many years, as that reply saved us from halving our share with Root and Scoot.

We became more and more concerned about the undue influence that Bona and Ringrose were having on Keith. We warned him on more than one occasion that they were starting to wag his tail. He chose to ignore us. He undoubtedly distrusted our motives and felt the need for his own organisation to counter us. We felt so strongly about this that we seriously discussed the possibility of approaching the Salvage Association for permission to proceed without JMRL.

We were becoming increasingly suspicious of the true motives of Bona and Ringrose. Ringrose seemed to trade solely off the fact that he had served on the minesweeper HMS *Bronington* under Prince Charles. It was about this time that Bona asked us if we would contribute toward a charitable fund

The Dammtor *on location April 1981.*
(Photo by M. Stewart)

that he was setting up for charities approved by Prince Charles. Malcolm and I had the strong feeling that if Prince Charles was at all human he probably felt the same way about Ringrose as we did. We promptly told Bona to bugger off. We were putting our personal fortunes on the line and charity begins at home. Who was going to come and bail us out when things went wrong and we were selling our homes to pay the costs of the expedition?

Again, we warned Keith that he was losing control of JMRL and should dump Bona and Ringrose. Again he refused, believing that he needed them to make his operation look credible. We could only imagine the bill that Bona would be abel to submit. If he was paid by the line, his verbosity would make him a millionaire.

OSA had appointed John Clarke as their project manager. This was a very

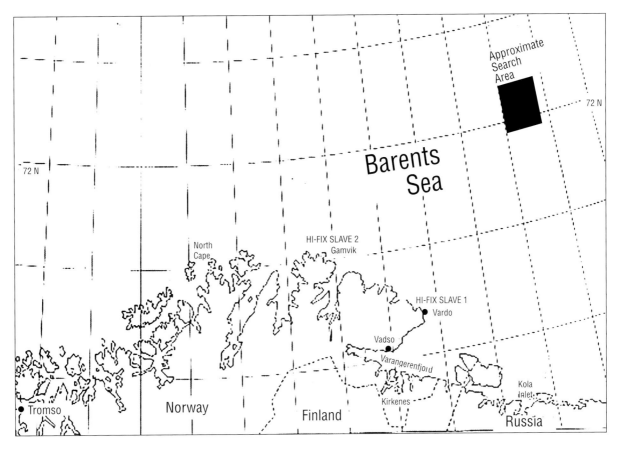

A map showing the approximate search area and proximal countries.

good move. We knew him and found him honest and straightforward to deal with. For our part, we contracted Mike Stewart as our project manager on the basis that he would run the operation offshore in all respects. Mike was also a formal naval officer who has been a clearance diver experienced in bomb and mine disposal under water. He was well-respected in the diving industry and Malcolm and I knew him as a man of impeccable honesty and integrity. We were both flat-out running a complex and demanding business. For us, Mike was the perfect man in whom to place our trust.

It is interesting that both Mike and John, as former naval officers, had the same opinion as Malcolm and I of Ringrose and would not give him the time of day.

Finally, the Soviet approval came through. It was the end of April 1981. We had already started to mobilise the *Dammtor* in Peterhead, and sailed on April 30. Thirty-nine years ago to the day, the *Edinburgh* was fighting for her life in the hostile waters of the Barents Sea. Accompanying us were John Clarke (representing our consortium as a surveyor and as a project manager for the search) and Ringrose (representing JMRL). Igor Illyn represented Ingostrach and joined the *Dammtor* on-site from a Russian tug.

This phase of the operation was efficiently led by John Clarke, with assistance from Kip Punch from Racal Decca whose job it was to locate the wreck. The 2W "Scorpio" ROV was on board with a full 2W support team. Racal Decca had a full spread of survey equipment including side scan sonar and the Hi-Fix ranging system. Those were the days before the advent of satellite positioning, and the most accurate navigation was still provided by the Decca chain. This was a land-based survey system that was based on an offshore receiver picking up signals from at least three shore-based radio stations that emitted permanent signals. The offshore unit could electronically triangulate the received data and provide a latitude and longitude position for the vessel to within an accuracy of about 30 metres (100 feet).

The problem in the Arctic has always been the lack of shore stations. To overcome this, Racal Decca had already sent out surveyors on cross-country skis in northern Norway to set up two temporary shore stations at Gamrik and Hardo with 20-metre towers and 100-watt transmitters to enable Kip to get an accurate position fix. He wanted to put a third station in Russia to get a better signal, but the Soviets would not allow it. It took a week for the *Dammtor* to make the passage around the Norwegian coast to the search area.

While waiting for the shore stations to be installed, *Dammtor* called at Kirkenes for stores and to pick up John Clarke. John started to survey using the Decca Chain but, as expected, it proved to be too inaccurate.

By now, John Clarke was convinced that the *Harrier's* position would prove to be the most accurate, while Kip and John Ringrose favoured the positions given by the Norwegian fishing vessels. Fortunately John's view prevailed. Keith, who for some strange reason had declined to go on the survey trip, had given Kip his best estimate of the position. This turned out to be more than 25 miles out!

Arriving at the *Harrier's* location, Kip paid out the transponder unit of the side scan sonar astern of the *Dammtor* and started a systematic box search of the area. Using this technology, a square area was set up on the chart, perhaps two miles by two miles, and the survey ship steamed precise parallel

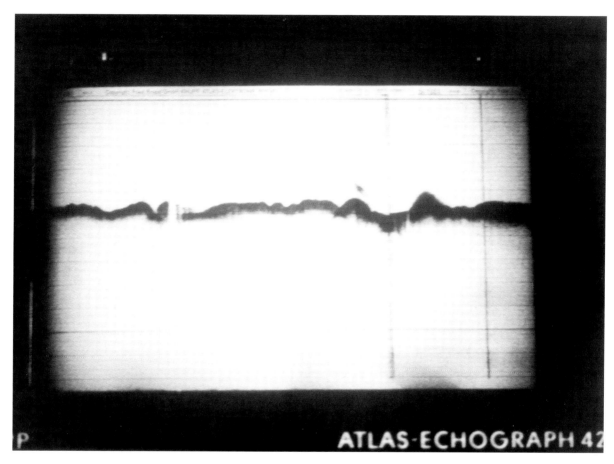

P

ATLAS-ECHOGRAPH 42

The echo sounder trace of the wreck of HMS Edinburgh.
(Photo by J. Clarke)

lines across the area. These lines are designed to overlap the range of the side scan sonar so as not to miss any targets.

The transit lines of the survey vessel are precisely plotted on a chart of the area so that the surveyors can make sure that no part of the area has been missed.

Incredibly, within an hour of starting the first run, a large trace appeared on the sonar. Kip confirmed that it was definitely a large wreck. On the *Dammtor*, excitement rose to fever pitch. To find a target so quickly was unheard of. But was it the *Edinburgh*, or our old friend *Hermann Shoemann the German*, or perhaps the ill-fated *Trinidad*? The wreck was plotted on the

Dammtor's sonar and found to be lying in a southwest/northeast direction on a relatively flat bottom in about 255 metres (840 feet) of water.

The reported sinking position of the *Edinburgh* was 71 51N 35 08E. The actual location of the mystery wreck is 71 04.37N 35 01.55E. This is some 15 miles north of the position given and vindicated John Clarke's analysis of the data that we had.

Feverish preparations were made to lower the "Scorpio" to the wreck site. As the first dive of the "Scorpio" was made the weather picked up. By the time the "Scorpio" neared the seabed the weather had deteriorated to such an extent that the superintendent aborted the dive and brought the "Scorpio" back to the surface. Malcolm and I had just invested one million dollars in the "Scorpio" which was then the last word in ROV technology. The "Scorpio" was insured, but Malcolm and I had to pay the first quarter of a million dollars if we lost it, and the lead time to replace it was more than six months. Needless to say, this had been drilled into the crew endlessly, and they were erring on the side of caution, which was fine by us!

We knew that the wreck had been snagged by fishermen several times and would be covered with abandoned nets. Together with all the masts and antennae of the wreck, these would make it a very dangerous place for an ROV. All ROVs are linked to the surface by an umbilical that provides power for its thrusters and cables for lights, TV cameras, and control of its manipulators (mechanical arms). The most likely cause of an entanglement would be the manipulator or the umbilical snagging on an obstruction. To minimise that danger, we had fixed the "Scorpio's" camera to look straight down. Normally it looks forward and can be scanned from side to side and up and down. By fixing it vertically down, we could stay above the wreck and hopefully see any snags before getting caught in them.

As soon as the weather subsided the *Dammtor* was repositioned over the site and the "Scorpio" was sent down again. John and the captain had great difficulty holding the vessel on station as it had only one anchor and, in that depth of water, the vessel would swing a long way at anchor. The "Scorpio"'s black and white camera sent back eerie grey images of plankton and occasional fish attracted by the vehicle's lights.

Then, at 245 metres (800 feet) down, a massive darker grey shape emerged. Obviously man-made, it was a large warship lying on its port side. There was an awed silence in the control room. Whichever ship it was, they were the first to see it for 39 years. A meticulous video inspection of the wreck was conducted. It was obvious that the

The crowded deck of the Dammtor. *(Photo by J. Clarke)*

seabed adjacent to the keel was clear of debris while the other side was too cluttered to risk inspection with the ROV. This information triggered considerable speculation as to the use of the wreck in post-war years.

We had learned on good advice that the US Navy had been using the wreck of the *Edinburgh* during their cold war surveillance of the Soviet navy's nuclear submarine fleet. Tracking the Soviet submarines relies primarily on recording the noise or "signature" made by their propellers. The US Navy had laid out long series of underwater listening devices to record the passage of hostile submarines in key narrows such as the Denmark Straight. Provided they knew the signature of an individual submarine, they could track its passage when on patrol.

The surveillance satellites could spot and identify the Soviet submarines leaving the Red Banner Fleet bases in the Kola Peninsula before they submerged. The U.S. Navy then used one of their submarines silently listening on the bottom to record the "signature" of the soviet submarine as it passed. We knew from our surveys that the seabed alongside the keel of the *Edinburgh* was clear of debris and that it would be possible to park a submarine there which, next to such a large mass of steel, would have been undetectable by the Soviet submarines. We understood that the US Navy was reluctant for the salvage attempt to proceed, perhaps concerned that their activities may be detected.

The operators now proceeded to fly the "Scorpio" along the starboard deck railing. The first surprise was a perfectly preserved, 32-foot-long Admiralty-pattern naval cutter, clinker built, still hanging in its davits. The paint was brilliant white, as if it had been painted the year before. This whaler ruled out our friend *Hermann Shoemann the German*, but it could still have belonged to the *Trinidad*. Moving forward along the railing the next object that loomed into view was a large single torpedo launching tube, again Admiralty pattern, but this too could have belonged to either the *Edinburgh* or the *Trinidad*. The silence in the control cabin was deafening as the "Scorpio" continued forward along the deck. The next image

took some seconds to sink in. They were looking at a vertical lattice work stanchion coming up from the deck to support the deck above the torpedo launching tube. It was the proof we had all been waiting for. They were looking down on the *Edinburgh*, and the grave of the 57 brave men who went with her on her final dive. There was noisy elation in the control room, and word was passed to us in code back in Aberdeen by land line from Tromso to announce the expedition's success.

The camera continued along the deck, clearly showing the steam catapult used to launch the Walrus aircraft and various fairleads and damaged handrailings.

As they filmed toward the forward turrets, no one at the time realised that the entire bridge structure was missing. This was to cause Malcolm and I immense heartache and very nearly caused us to cancel the project. Forward of the missing bridge, the camera filmed the base of "A" turret and then moved up and filmed the three 6-inch guns of "A" turret still pointing over the starboard bow where they were fired shortly before she sank.

The camera continued right to the bow where it showed a large split in the hull running down from the deck level. This perplexed us as we had no record of any damage to the bow section. We eventually worked out that this split had been caused by the weight of anchor chain in the bow chain lockers, which caused the hull to crack open.

When large ships are built, the transverse girders that carry the outer skin of the vessel are known as frames. The frames are numbered going astern from the bow. We were particularly interested in frame 93. At this frame, there was a strengthened transverse watertight bulkhead (wall) across the ship. This was where the deck level stepped up one deck to the higher portion of the bow and the base of the bridge structure. Frame 93 was also the stern of the bridge structure and, more importantly, the aft bulkhead of the bomb room.

The "Scorpio" flew back to the torpedo launcher, just forward of frame 93 to look for the damage caused by the first torpedo strike. The damage was shocking. There was an almost square hole big enough to drive a bus through. The torpedo had hit the lower section of the ships armour plating, ripping out a complete sheet of the armour and opening up a massive hole into the compartment beyond, which was a very large tank for the furnace fuel oil used to power the *Edinburgh's* engines.

The crew filmed as much as they reasonably could and then sailed back in triumph to Peterhead. John Clarke gave us a detailed briefing back in the office as soon as they arrived. The future of the project now fell squarely on the shoulders of 2W. At the end of the day, it was up to Malcolm and I to underwrite the project, and we had to be totally sure that a salvage was feasible.

We locked ourselves away with Mike Stewart and John Clarke and looked at all the videos dozens of times. The good news was that there had been no previous salvage attempt. We were on virgin territory. Bonham-Carter's report to the Admiralty had said that, after the final torpedo strike on the port side, "The ship was open from side to side." As he witnessed her sinking from the bridge of the *Harrier*, he made notes and was later to report to the Admiralty, "The ship had had all she could take. She rolled over to port, her back broken, and the last seen of her was her bows rising vertically in the air and the disappearing. The after part just rolled over."

This very clearly gave the impression that the ship had broken into two parts. We could see no sign of this on the videos. It is very unfair for someone who was not even born at the time to criticise an officer who was out there risking his life with the rest of the crew. However, we were beginning to feel that Bonham-Carter's account of events may have contained more than a little journalistic licence, perhaps to explain his subsequently questioned decision to abandon ship.

We could see no deformation in the ship's hull to suggest that her back was broken. We had not, however, been able to look at the port side, or at the keel below the bomb room. Therefore, we did not know whether we would cut through the starboard side of the hull and find ourselves looking at the seabed, or whether the keel was blown away in that area and all our gold had been deposited far away on the seabed.

We knew that Max Teichert in U-456 had fired a salvo of three torpedoes at the *Edinburgh.* Two had struck simultaneously, one just forward and below the bomb room and one in the stern, also on the starboard side. We had copies of the original damage reports from the ship. The first torpedo had stuck approximately 20 feet forward of the bomb room. The force of the explosion had burst through into a small arms store and a provisions store, and, more tragically, into the seamen's and stoker's mess deck where many lives had been lost. It had also burst upwards into a machine shop that was built above the fuel tank, causing further loss of men working in that area. The damage-control parties had closed all the watertight doors in that area to prevent further flooding. In the process, they had trapped a young seaman in a communications compartment. There was no way of getting him out without risking loss of the ship. The Captain spoke to him several times on the ship's telephone system before his air finally ran out.

As previously stated, warships such as the *Edinburgh* are narrow and designed to cut through the water at speed. They have a great deal of weight above decks with the massive gun turrets and so have little reserves of stability, particularly when damaged. There was a standard instruction for the crew that in the event of torpedo damage and the ship developing a list, all available crew were to move to the high side of the ship to counteract the list. This may sound silly, but the combined weight of the *Edinburgh's* crew was more than 50 tons.

The flooding from this first torpedo caused an immediate list to starboard, which was corrected by flooding opposite compartments on the port side. When this was completed, the ship was some ten feet lower in the water, a fact that was to be of great significance in the final outcome. While all this damage control work was underway, injured crewmen were being brought up from the seamen's and stoker's mess deck. Captain Faulkner began to realise the full extent of the damage done by the second of Max Teichert's torpedoes that had hit the stern. This was the crippling blow. When the two explosions occurred, almost simultaneously, the crew described it "As if the ship had been gripped in a giant hand and shaken." She immediately slowed and slewed to starboard. Looking aft, the complete afterdeck had been blown up and bent over the barrels of "Y" turret. The gun barrels were actually poking through the twisted deck plating. Shortly afterwards, with a violent shudder, the stern separated completely and sank, taking with it both rudders and both main propellers and shafts. With the weight of this section of the stern missing, the ship was now some eight feet down by the head.

It remains a mystery to me why, with the ship stopped and the destroyer escorts still miles away, Teichert did not move in to finish her off instead of shadowing her for the next two days. He must have thought that the damage was so extensive she would sink anyway without the further expenditure of torpedoes.

The *Edinburgh* had four engines and four separate shafts and propellers. It was the main propellers at the stern of the vessel that were severed. The auxiliary shafts and propellers were outboard of the mains and further forward. These were undamaged by the explosion.

We were sure the damage at the stern would not have affected the bomb room, but we had to be sure that the first torpedo had not blown out the bottom of the ship. From a detailed study of the damage reports and the plans of the vessel we had obtained, we deduced that, at this stage, the bomb room would have been largely intact, but full of water. This confirmed the information in Bonham-Carter's signal to the Admiralty that "the gold was in a compartment flooded by the first torpedo."

At the very end of the engagement, the German destroyer Z 24 had fired a fan of torpedoes at the *Edinburgh*. Faulkner saw them coming and tried to turn *Edinburgh* toward them in the hope that they would pass harmlessly down each side of the vessel. Low in the water and with only her auxiliary engines her response was sluggish. She was still in a hard turn to port when one of the torpedoes hit her amidships on the port side sending a column of water up over the bridge. This was when Bonham Carter reported that "she was open from side to side," meaning that this third torpedo had blown through into the hole formed by the first hit.

Malcolm and I sat for hours alternately re-running all the videos and studying the damage reports. Our elation at finding the wreck was rapidly evaporating. The whole team had been on a high since the discovery, and everyone was mentally gearing up for a salvage operation that summer. The problem was that, at the end of the project, it was Malcolm and I who were to underwrite the operation. We had already personally paid for the entire cost of the survey, except for the OSA vessel and the Racal Decca expenses. We were under no illusions as to what a full-scale salvage would cost. We had to be completely sure that the gold was still there, and that a salvage was technically feasible before we put our homes on the line.

We were fortunate that the wreck lay in just over 244 metres (800 feet) of water. Had it been over 305 metres (1,000 feet) we would have called off the operation. That depth was beyond the limits of diving technology at that time. As it was, we were already extremely worried about a depth of 244 metres. The deepest working dives in the North Sea at that time had only been to 122 metres (400 feet). Comex had put divers down to 457 metres (1,500 feet) during experimental dives in chambers, but there had been no working dives to 244 metres, and certainly none in waters so cold and hostile.

If Bonham-Carter was to be believed, and the ship had been opened from side to side, then we were clearly wasting our time, as the gold would be scattered in a trail across the bottom of the Barents Sea. I had already formed a poor opinion of Bonham-Carter; perhaps unfairly, as he was already dead and I had not had the opportunity to meet him. We knew that he was wrong about the ship breaking her back as she sank. If the ship was opened up so far down in the hull then her keel would have been blown out and she would have broken her back. On balance, we felt that this was unlikely. We suspected that Bonham-Carter would have sought to justify his abandonment of the vessel at that time, when many felt that he should have stayed with her and continued the effort to get her back to Murmansk. We had pretty well convinced ourselves that the bomb room was probably still largely intact when she sank, but we were now faced with a much more worrisome problem.

It was abundantly clear from the video that the entire bridge structure was missing, broken cleanly off at deck level. We knew from survivor's accounts that it had been in place when the vessel sank, so it must have come off as a result of the impact with the seabed. In fact, we never found the bridge structure and must assume that it is lying detached, somewhere near the vessel. Our concern now centred on how violent the impact with the seabed had been. With dummy boxes, we calculated how big the stack of gold would have been in the bomb room, and how high its centre of gravity would have been above the floor. Our engineers now calculated the forces that would be required for the gold to rip through the bulkhead into the compartment directly astern. We knew from Risdon Beazley's experience with the *Empire Manor* that gold, being so heavy, does break through bulkheads when a ship hits the bottom. Frame 93 was the bulkhead at the stern of the bomb room;

directly behind that lay a magazine for the main 6-inch guns. We studied the *Belfast* and found that this is a large compartment full of racking to hold the shells from floor to ceiling. We knew that to extract the gold from there would be immensely time consuming and economically impossible.

I set about trying to find out what happens when a big ship sinks and exactly how hard they hit the bottom. Surprisingly, no one seemed to know. I spoke to Surgeon Commander Rawlins in the Royal Navy who had been involved in researching how ditched aircraft sink. He told me they usually "glide" down under water and touch down gently, the right way up, although they occasionally nose-dive vertically into the seabed at great speed. This did not really help very much, and no one else seemed to have any information on the subject. The *Empire Manor* had nose-dived into the sea bed, but in much shallower water. The *Edinburgh*, weighing 10,000 tons, was 183 metres (600 feet) long and sank in just over 244 metres (800 feet) of water. We know that she left the surface vertically, stern first, at which point her damaged stern would have been some 61 metres (200 feet) above the seabed. Ten thousand tons falling 61 metres (200 feet) into the sea bed would certainly have ripped off the bridge and sent the gold flying through several bulkheads. Yet there was contradictory evidence that perplexed us.

The heavy clinker built cutter was still hanging in its davits with its wire rope falls. Why had that not been ripped off? Further along the deck was the starboard torpedo launching tube, a heavy installation on a relatively slender pivoting pedestal. Why was the pedestal not bent by the impact with the seabed?

We clearly had a lot more homework to do before we could safely proceed. Considering that the ship was abandoned very soon after the third torpedo strike, we were very surprised to find a detailed, typed report of that damage in the Public Records Office. Malcolm and I pored over that report for hours analysing every statement in it.

There was a reference to the deck behind the bridge "petalling" up with the force of the explosion. Captain Faulkner had also referred to this in his reports. This was strange as there was no such report of decks "petalling" or peeling up as a result of the first torpedo. Slowly it dawned on us and we began to piece together what had happened. After the first explosion, not only the bomb room area was flooded, but also the lower compartments on the port side. The vessel was now some 3 metres (10 feet) lower in the water and was heeling sharply to port when the third torpedo struck. It must therefore have struck the ship much higher up than the first.

In common with other cruisers, the *Edinburgh* had an armoured deck above the waterline to prevent bombs penetrating into the heart of the ship. It is clear that the third torpedo struck at, or above this level. Water is incompressible, and with all the lower compartments in that area already flooded, the force of the explosion took the path of least resistance, which was up. Hence the "petalling" of the deck behind the bridge and the undoubted weakening of the bridge foundations.

Inside the stern of the bridge at deck level was a large hanger to house the Walrus aircraft. As the ship sank stern first, the air in this hanger would have been trapped and rapidly compressed as the ship sank. It was probably this force, coupled with the weakened foundations that caused the bridge to ripped off before the vessel even hit the bottom.

Subsequent evidence seems to indicate that that ships sink through the water like a leaf falling in air. The *Edinburgh* must have glided quite gently into the bottom during the first part of her descent. In very deep water wrecks accelerate and, in cases like the *Titanic*, actually snap in half when the forces of acceleration exceed the strength of the hull. This is the same mechanism that causes tall chimneys to break in half on the way down when they are demolished.

Even having satisfactorily explained the missing bridge, we were still certain that the gold would have moved through the bulkhead at frame 93 and were not prepared to go ahead. We had for sometime now been tracing and interviewing survivors. All those that we contacted were universally supportive and helpful, and intrigued to see the videos of their old ship. About this time I had made contact with one survivor who had been an ordinary seaman on *Edinburgh* and was now a wealthy banker in Paris. That made me a bit suspicious, had he got off with any of the gold? His mother had been French and he spoke the language fluently and had therefore been in the working party that had loaded the gold. I flew him to Aberdeen and showed him the videos. Over lunch his amazing story came out. He had survived the *Edinburgh* sinking and then been sent home in the *Trinidad*. He had survived that sinking and, after a long and miserable wait in Murmansk, he was returned to the UK in an armed trawler. He was landed at Glasgow where he phoned his mother in London from a public call box, three months after he had been reported missing, presumed dead. He was then sent to the Mediterranean where he survived a third sinking on the Malta convoys.

I questioned him in detail about his role in loading the gold. He had been in the party on deck, but had been sent down to the bomb room to help when the case of gold had been dropped and broken open. He had then helped load the cases into the bomb room. With bated breath I asked him how he stacked them. "Christ," he said, "they were far too heavy, we just dragged them in and spread them out over the floor, then we stacked the bomb trolleys and paravane wires on top of them."

Having seen him off at the airport with profuse thanks, I rushed back to the office to pass this news on to Malcolm and Mike. This meant that the centre of gravity of the gold was about three inches above the floor and the heel of the bulkhead (where it joined the floor) was strengthened. Our engineers redid their calculations and came back with the conclusion that the bulkhead would have held.

It was on that day, and based on that vital information, that we decided to go ahead with a salvage attempt and moved the organisation into high gear. We invited the management of OSA over to Aberdeen to view the video and discuss the program. They brought with them one of their senior captains, and a wartime veteran of Kriegsmarine. As we watched the video and the camera panned down to look at the torpedo hole the OSA captain just about broke off anglo-german relations by commenting "foking good our torpedoes, ja!" Fortunately, he was not to be the captain of the *Stephaniturm*.

Now that we had made the decision to go, it was already well into May of 1981 and we wanted to sail in September to get the best of the weather. The *Stephaniturm* was on charter to our erstwhile employer Comex, but was due to be released in mid-July, which would suit us fine and give us adequate time for preparation. Prior to mobilisation, the *Stephaniturm* was to have a complete technical audit of the diving system (which was rated to 796 metres [1,300 feet]) to ensure that all certification was up to date and all cables were of the correct length. All the life support umbilical bundles were to be renewed and extra insulated hot-water umbilicals were to be provided.

Mike Stewart's planning was meticulous and thorough. He had carefully chosen his superintendent Mike O'Meara (also a Royal Navy clearance diver) who had the enviable reputation of being one of the most experienced saturation diving supervisors in the North Sea. He and Mike chose his life-support and deck crew, and together they and Malcolm set about selecting the best of the world's deep divers for this record-breaking operation.

While Malcolm and Mike pushed ahead with the technical preparations, I concentrated on the financing and trying to shut up Bona, who was still driving us mad. We already had the ship and the survey input as part of our consortium. One major item of cost was to be the helium gas for the saturation divers. I approached our gas supplier, Gas and Equipment, owned by Ron Billington and Leon Metcalfe, with the proposal that they supply all the gas on a no cure, no pay basis. I suggested a scheme that, if we failed they got nothing, but if we succeeded they got six times the value of the gas multiplied by the percentage of the five and a half tons of gold that we recovered. They agreed to this, and I used that formula as the basis for other no cure no pay deals.

The *Stephaniturm* suffered from having a very small deck area. It soon became apparent that there would not be enough space to store all the gas we would need. An American living in Aberdeen named Don Rodocker, had just developed an innovative gas-recovery system. This used a special helmet from which the diver's exhaled gas was returned to the surface and purified by removing the carbon dioxide. Oxygen was then added to make the correct mixture and the gas was repressurised and returned to the diver. It sounds easy now, but back then this was a revolutionary development. We agonised long and hard whether we should take the risk of trying a new development on such a high-risk job. We knew Don and had great faith in his technical ability. After trials conducted by both Mikes, we decided to give it a try, with the fallback that we could go back onto

open circuit if it was not working correctly. That would mean an expensive re-supply job in mid-operation. Don knew that, if this job was successful, it would make his name. He agreed therefore to come for his basic costs only.

We had to have a high level of liability insurance for the divers. This has always been very expensive and could be almost unobtainable for such a deep operation. I approached our old friend Michael Payne, a leading and highly respected underwriter at Lloyds who already insured our North Sea operations. He was a bit taken aback with my suggestion of no cure, no pay for the insurance premium, but he soon warmed to the idea and it became a Lloyds "first." The terms of the insurance cover were as follows:

1) A cash deposit premium paid prior to sailing based on the normal salaries of the divers.
2) In the event of no recovery and no claims the deposit premium to be repaid.
3) If no recovery and claims in excess of the deposit premium then the deposit to be doubled.
4) If bullion was recovered with no claims, then a five times multiplier to be applied to the premium.
5) If bullion was recovered, but claims were in excess of the deposit premium then the multiplier would be ten.

I was still very concerned about the amount of cash outlay that Malcolm and I were committing to that was not covered by no cure, no pay deals. So I set about looking for some cash investors on the same deal of six to one multiplied by the percentage of gold that we recovered. Much to my surprise, I only managed to find two who both subsequently became wealthy and grateful. After the event, dozens of people said that they would have invested, but hindsight is always 20/20.

Mike was now getting down to the fine details, optimistically manufacturing steel cages with which to raise the gold and even bags for lifting bars. We did not expect any of the wooden gold boxes to have survived in sound condition, so the bars would have to be lifted in our specially-built containers.

We were beginning to finalise the crew list for the *Stephaniturm*. With only 60 bunks over and above the accommodation for the ship's crew, space was severely restricted. Keith insisted on going even though he could only be an observer at this stage. Malcolm and I decided not to go as we still had a business to run and we were really needed to provide back up support in Aberdeen. The Ministry of Defence was to send David Keogh as their representative and the Soviets were sending Igor Illyn and Leonid Melodinsky, who we believe was Igor's KGB minder.

Don Roedoker was going to supervise the use of his equipment and we had extra mechanical and electrical technicians and tons of spare parts.

Keith, convinced that we would succeed was organising his own publicity and wanted to bring a journalist along. He had phoned the *Sunday Times* to offer them the story and the phone had been answered by Barrie Penrose. Penrose had achieved fame, or rather notoriety, by writing the book that exposed Jeremy Thorpe. I do not believe that he was actually employed by the *Sunday Times* at the time, but was working in their office on an assignment. He jumped at this opportunity and latched on to Keith like a leech.

Malcolm and I did not want any journalists on board at all. We were going into uncharted territory at world record depth and the last thing we wanted if we had a diving accident was a reporter writing up the gory details. We had blazing rows with Keith on the subject, and warned him that, if there was any adverse publicity, we would pull the plug and ban communications from the ship. Sadly for Keith, he prevailed and Penrose joined the crew. Also with him was the *Sunday Times* photographer Paul Berrif, and Ian Yeomans, who was also to take the three colour photos of each bar recovered that the principals were demanding.

We now turned our attention to security. Although we would effectively be in Soviet water, the world knew that we were going after the gold. So, we had to have some form of code system. In those days, there were no satellite phone links. We would have to rely on single-sideband radio phone connections to and from the ship which would not be secure lines. We had all been referring to the whole project as operation "Greyhound" for some months, but now needed a more detailed security procedure.

Bona got in on the act and produced a complete bound code book that was so laughable we used it. It was all to do with dogs. Bona was "Kennel" and his secretary Brenda was "Kennelmaid." David Keogh was "Henry," after his red setter, and Keith was "Sam," after his terrier. For some inexplicable reason, each message was to begin with "Keeper" and end with "Collar."

There was then a list of numbers that referred to phrases in the code books to transmit important information in code. It had been expanded from a shorter version used on the survey operation. This part of the code system was useful:

Dog 1   The Russians are becoming a problem.
Dog 2   The situation in the bomb room area is.....
Dog 3   The wreck is upright.
Dog 4   The wreck is upside down.
Dog 5   We have found a large wreck.
Dog 6   The wreck has collapsed.
Dog 7   The wreck is on its port side.
Dog 8   The wreck is on its starboard side.
Dog 9   We are unable to determine the situation regarding the bomb room.
Dog 10 The wreck has collapsed in the area of the bomb room.
Dog 11 Do you wish us to mark the wreck with a transponder?
Dog 12 The situation looks impossible.
Dog 13 Bottom conditions are good.
Dog 14 We anticipate completion in — days.
Dog 15 This part of the wreck is underneath and cannot be seen.
Dog 16 There are no nets in the area.
Dog 17 The bomb room is intact inside the wreck.
Dog 18 We have found the *Hermann Schoemann.*
Dog 19 The wreck is in one piece.
Dog 20 The wreck is in pieces.
Dog 21 We are returning to port because of Dog 1.
Dog 22 Conditions inside the wreck are —.
Dog 23 The underwater camera is u/s.
Dog 24 Please call the ship.
Dog 25 Everything looks OK.
Dog 26 We are returning to port.
Dog 27 The tide is a problem.
Dog 28 The location is marked with a transponder
Dog 29 We have found the stern section.

Dog 30 We have found the bow section.
Dog 31 The bomb room is broken open.
Dog 32 Bottom conditions are bad.
Dog 33 The underwater camera is working.
Dog 34 I will return and report.
Dog 35 There are nets in area.
Dog 36 We have found the gold.
Dog 37 We are having no problems with the Russians.
Dog 38 The tide is not a problem.
Dog 39 Visibility in the area is bad.
Dog 40 Visibility in the area is good.

There was a more exhaustive list dealing with diving problems, but all we wanted to hear was "Dog 36." This was to be followed by Greek numbers to indicate the total number of bars recovered.

This code system was to be the source of much amusement to us and embarrassment to Bona as the job got underway.

Malcolm and I now had to address a more serious matter. We sat for hours with Mike Stewart and Mike O'Meara planning how we would get into the wreck. The video showed the gaping hole in the side leading into the dark void of the starboard fuel tank. We knew the fuel tank to be 12 feet wide at this point, its inner wall being the outer wall of a store room and a small arms magazine at that point. Some 20 feet astern from the torpedo hole, the inner wall of the fuel tank was the outer wall of the bomb room. The bomb room was 16 feet by 16 feet across and the inner corridor was where the gold had been lowered in Murmansk. This corridor was on the centre line of the ship. Across this corridor from the bomb room was an identical room used to store fuses. It was extremely fortunate for us that the ship was on its port side. Had it been the other way up, it is doubtful that we could have proceeded owing to the extra distance that we would have had to excavate.

Our obvious route in was through the torpedo hole, working our way astern 20 feet and cutting through the outer wall of the bomb room. Our reserve approach would be to cut through the hull immediately above the bomb room. We commissioned a detailed model of the section of the ship around the bomb room from original plans obtained by John Clarke. The model was made of perspex and was complete with gold boxes made to the same scale. Subsequently, it was kept in the saturation chambers throughout the diving operations so the divers could plan their work and mark up what they had done on the model. John Clarke also made up a folder of all relevant plans for the divers and supervisors. These plans and the model proved to be of great value and saved a lot of diving time and effort.

Our problem centred around the cut that would have to be made into the bomb room. We knew that the fuel tank was flooded and that, if we had to, we could safely cut through the outer skin of that above the bomb room. If the bomb room's outer wall was intact, then there was a serious risk of a build-up of explosive gases behind it. The bomb room contained a variety of bombs for the Walrus aircraft, each weighing up to 500 pounds. The room also contained numerous fuses and other explosives. Over the years, these may have started to decompose and cause a build up of explosive gases. We could not risk letting a diver put an oxyarc burning rod through a sealed bulkhead. (There had just been a serious accident in the North Sea in which a diver had done just that. The resulting explosion shattered his face mask. It was only by the quick actions of his partner in the diving bell that his life was saved.)

One way to overcome this problem is to use what is called a "trepanning charge." This is a small circular-shaped explosive charge that is placed on the bulkhead. When fired, it cuts a neat circular hole in the metal. The problem was we had been awarded the contract based on a controlled entry by divers, as opposed to the blast and grab method. Even though such a charge would only do the same work as a diver with a cutting torch, we felt that its use could be blown out of all proportions as an emotive issue.

Bomb Fuses - shell cases and Cordite.
(Photo by M. Stewart)

On a strictly need-to-know basis we explained our dilemma to the MoD. They were very helpful and sent David Keogh to witness a secret demonstration of the latest system that used liquid explosives. The components came in two separate containers and were completely inert until mixed. These were duly shipped on board the *Stephaniturm* accompanied by an explosives expert, Dr. Sydney Alford. He also could comment on the stability of the munitions the divers would have to disturb in the bomb room. Five members of the team were former Royal Navy bomb and mine disposal experts from the clearance dive branch.

During the period of waiting for the salvage to get underway, Keith was desperate for money. We had already sent him out to work as a diving supervisor on one of our contracts in India, but that was not enough to pay the mounting bills he must have been getting from Bona. He approached Malcolm and I for a loan and we agreed to advance him funds at the rate of £1,500 per month to be repaid from the salvage proceeds. This was just piling up the risks for us as we could not see Keith ever paying it back if the salvage failed.

It was now well into July and Comex were showing no signs of releasing the *Stephaniturm*. Henri Delauze was pretty upset that we had found the wreck and had the salvage contract. We were suspicious that he was using his financial muscle to keep the boat until it was too late in the season for us to mobilise. John Clarke personally went to see the managing director of Comex and told him that he would withdraw the *Stephaniturm* whether they liked it or not. After that acrimonious meeting, we got the vessel at the end of August, just in time for the September operation.

Saturation divers frequently suffer from a painful and very contagious ear infection called Pio, which breeds in the high-pressure, humid environment of saturation chambers and is very infectious. It has long been a politically incorrect joke in the industry that French divers suffer from it more due to a lower standard of personal hygiene. This may be unfair to our French brethren because, although the diving chambers were meticulously cleaned before they went into use, we sure had problems with the Pio bug in the *Stephaniturm's* chambers. Perhaps it was a parting gift from Comex, who were still smarting about Malcolm and I leaving them to set up our own business and beating them to the *Edinburgh*.

The Soviets now decided that they would have to make another visit to Aberdeen to "approve" the *Stephaniturm* before we left. This seemingly had more to do with a jolly to the west than a serious technical assessment. The *Stephaniturm* was apparently light years ahead of anything that they had.

At about this time we were struck with a bombshell in the shape of the VAT office who contacted me to ask how I proposed to pay the VAT on the gold that I was planning to import. Having already laboriously negotiated a contract in which the government already got 55% of the proceeds for no expenditure, here they were asking for another

15% (the VAT rate at that time) of our share. The idea was so preposterous that we thought that they were joking. This was the start a chain of bureaucratic stupidity and ignorance at which the British Civil Service excel. Their sole aim seems to be to destroy initiative, and drive entrepreneurs and wealth generators to more receptive pastures overseas.

My accountants could not believe they were serious either, so a meeting was set up at the Customs and Excise VAT head office in London. There were three of us and they brought 15 people to the meeting to justify their case. As I looked around the table in disbelief I was reminded if Alfred Hitchcock's famous film "The Birds." The vultures had started to gather in earnest, their beaks dripping with saliva. They flapped their wings and ruffled their feathers, eyeing me up as their next meal.

"No," they said, "it's definitely a gold import and VAT would be payable in cash or a banker's draft on import" (i.e., when *Stephaniturm* arrived in Peterhead).

They pointed out that if the governments paid us in cash there would be no VAT to pay. The Soviets had agreed to pay us in cash in London at the gold price ruling on the day we delivered their share to Murmansk. The British government, however, was giving us

our share in gold, and it would be in our possession at the time of import. If we got all the gold, our share from the UK alone would be over £6 million, giving a VAT bill of £1 million for the salvors.

"Does the British government pay VAT on the gold they import?" I asked.

"Oh no! They are exempt," was the reply.

"Well," I said, "why don't I get the government to import ours and pay me in cash?"

"Oh we could not allow that; the Exchequer would get less revenue," was the prompt reply.

"Well bugger the lot of you," I said with some feeling, "I will land the cargo in the Channel Islands where there is no VAT."

"I think we will be able to persuade the MoD to stop you from doing that," came the smug reply of officialdom.

I felt truly stretched out over a barrel, fixing to get rogered at both ends. I quickly retired with my advisers to discuss tactics. A quick call to the Salvage Association confirmed that we would not be allowed to land the gold at a port outside mainland Britain and the government wouldn't land our share of the gold and pay us cash. The bastards had moved fast to get their sticky fingers on an extra million pounds.

What really upset me was that we had not even sailed yet, nor found a bar of gold, and the "system" was already trying to take it from us. After a lot of hard research, we came up with a loophole that we could slip through. If we transferred ownership of the gold to a registered bullion dealer before importation he could then import it under the "postponed VAT accounting system". This meant that when he sold it on with VAT, he would account for the input VAT and we would get our money free of VAT.

I proceeded to do a deal with one of the major London bullion dealers, who will remain nameless (as they won't like what I have to say about them later). The deal meant that anyone wanting to keep a bar as a souvenir would have to pay the 15% VAT, the deal would only work if the ownership of the gold was passed on legally before arrival in the UK. It is interesting to note that, shortly after this, the postponed accounting treatment was scrapped after it was used by people fencing the gold stolen in the Brinksmat robbery. The only way now for anyone to avoid VAT on a salvage of bullion would be land it in a state where VAT does not apply.

The last problem that Malcolm and I had to address was how to prevent gold bars from being stolen by our own divers. We had plenty of poachers turned game keepers in 2W and an informal gathering of our ex-divers now in management soon came up with some 20 ways of stealing individual bars. As Malcolm rightly said, it is the 21st method we should worry about. Fortunately the bars were too big to be secreted in body cavities, but there were plenty of cavities around a diving bell that could hide one. The Soviets had already said that they wished their representatives to travel back to Aberdeen at the end of the job to inspect the inside of the chambers when the divers came out of saturation. A great deal of vigilance was going to be needed.

This seemed very unkind and unnecessary for such a professional crew who were all personally known to both Mikes. But Malcolm and I would have looked pretty silly with our insurers if we had not taken full precautions. In the event, as expected, nothing went missing in this phase of the operation.

On board the *Stephaniturm*, John Clarke converted the bosun's locker on the starboard side into an impromptu bullion room. It was fitted with three massive locks; one for the Russians, one for David Keogh, and one for 2W. No one could get in unless both principals and the salvor were present.

When things began to really come together, the Soviets dropped the next bombshell. They would not have enough sterling to pay us in cash, so they would pay us in gold as well. Thank God we had set up the postponed accounting system to avoid VAT, or the potential VAT bill for the salvage would now have been £3 million! There followed interminable meetings and telexes to decide how the gold would be divided in Murmansk. This was a heaven-sent opportunity for Bona to again exercise his verbosity. He managed to make a relatively simple matter very complicated. The problem with a physical division of bars in Murmansk was that it was certain that the amounts would not divide accurately to the nearest bar. The Soviets insisted that they would divide it to the nearest bar in their favour and later make a cash adjustment. To further complicate the matter OSA, JMRL, Racal Decca, and ourselves all required a physical split at that stage too, so that we could make individual transfers of ownership to bullion dealers to avoid the VAT.

It should be noted that all these events took place at the height of the Cold War, with a great deal of mutual suspicion between us and the Soviets. Malcolm and I had never been comfortable about going to Murmansk after the salvage. It would be all too easy for the Soviets to trump up some flimsy excuse to detain the vessel and confiscate our share of the gold. We felt a serious sense of responsibility to our risk-taking subcontractors and investors who were putting their trust in us.

I approached Michael Payne at Lloyds again to arrange for expropriation insurance to cover us for the full value of our share of the gold in the event of theft or of seizure by the Soviets. The premium of £70,000 was only to be payable once we had recovered the gold, effectively a no cure, no pay deal again. It turned out to be a waste of money, but it gave us great peace of mind and in the same situation, I would pay it again.

The Stephaniturm on site at night.
(Photo by J. Clarke)

The heroic diving team.
(Photo by M. Stewart)

*Loading extra helium gas
from a supply boat on site.
(Photo by J. Clarke)*

*The crowded conditions in
the diving bell showing the
coiled divers' umbilicals.
(Photo by M.Stewart)*

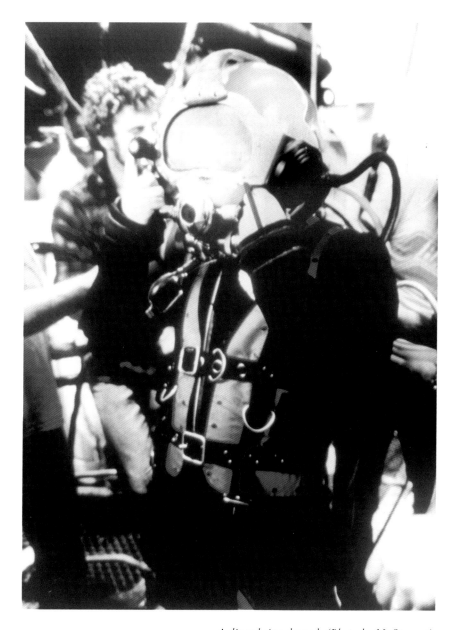

A diver being dressed. (Photo by M. Stewart)

The diving bell over the top of the Moonpool. (Photo by J. Clark)

The diving bell being launched in the Moonpool. The matching hatch to the saturation chambers at the top of the picture. (Photo by M. Stewart)

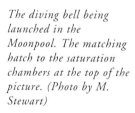

The crowded deck of the Dammtor.
(Photo by M. Stewart)

The loaded deck of the
Stephaniturm *prior to sailing.*
(Photo by J. Clarke)

*The cage bringing up
bars from the wreck.
(Photo by M. Stewart)*

*Sacks of gold ingots being
lifted on board.
(Photo by J. Clarke)*

Some of the crew with ingots and artifacts.
(Photo by M. Stewart)

The 2W owners. (Left to right) Ric Wharton, David Eliot, and Malcolm Williams. (Photo by R. Wharton)

STRIKING

GOLD

CHAPTER 6

It was now August 30, 1981, and *Stephaniturm* was finally ready to sail from Peterhead on her great adventure. It would be the culmination of years of hope and negotiation and many months of arduous planning and preparation. We were going off into the unknown, at depths never before attempted, in hostile waters, both physically and politically. We were extending our diving technology beyond the known limits, and putting the lives of our divers in peril for the pursuit of profit. Was it morally justifiable? Yes, I think it was. The divers were all volunteers and taking their share of the financial risks with us as well.

We had spared no expense to get the best equipment and specialists, our research had been thorough and our preparation meticulous. We had massive stocks of spares and supplies and as much equipment redundancy as could be fitted onto the *Stephaniturm*. We were now embarking on the diving equivalent of the first moonwalk. Similar to Apollo 1 lifting off for the moon, when *Stephaniturm* sailed from Peterhead, the crew was on its own and beyond the practical help of us back in Aberdeen. In common with the astronauts, we would only have radio communication, although less frequently, and certainly less confidentially.

Above, The fore end of the Stephaniturm. *(Photo by J. Clarke)*
opp. page: The aft end of the Stephaniturm. *(Photo by J. Clarke)*

The Stephaniturm's *Captain — Ronnie Goetz on the bridge. (Photo by J. Clarke)*

Just before the vessel sailed, Malcolm spoke to the assembled crew. He drew their attention to the risks and difficulties that we faced and particularly stressed that he did not want any unauthorised persons in the dive control shack where the supervisors worked. It was a very small room and their job was critical to the safety of the divers. Their attention must not be distracted by visitors and sightseers. The whole operation would be constantly filmed, and monitors had been set up in an adjoining room for non-essential personnel to watch and listen to what was going on.

As the ship pulled away from the quay in the early hours of the morning, there was a universal feeling of relief that all the fussing was at an end and they were now free of our interference and under their own command.

There was a strange split of command on the vessel, and it is a tribute to all concerned that they developed a *modus vivandi* that worked. The *Stephaniturm's* captain was Ronnie Goetz, a vastly experienced seaman and very helpful to the team. Normally, the captain of a ship is god at sea, but on a diving vessel, when divers are in the water, he must take orders from the Diving Superintendent, unless the safety of the vessel is in question. Mike O'Meara had the ultimate and legal responsibility for his divers and no one could override that.

Mike Stewart was in overall charge of the operation and the senior man on board. John Clarke was in a strange position; he was OSA's management representative, but not in the direct chain of command. In practice, their relationship worked well, as he and Mike Stewart were both former navy officers and knew and respected each other. In fact, they worked very closely together in the management of the overall

project and John's senior position in OSA enabled him to solve many practical difficulties for Mike on board before they became a real problem.

Keith Jessop was really along as a passenger. He had already done his job admirably and, as the father figure of the project, was allotted the charterer's cabin, an honour richly deserved for the man who had doggedly pursued the *Edinburgh* for so many years. Keith had the luxury of time to wander the ship and talk to everyone and watch his dream unfold. We had come a long way since that Saturday when he first came into my office. Everything he had said had been delivered and all that he had asked of me had been done.

Igor Illyn and Leon Melodinsky in the dive control room with Mike O'Meara. (Photo by J. Clarke)

David Keogh from the Ministry of Defence was the essence of the British gentleman, polite and helpful throughout; he understood and accepted his role as observer. The Soviet observers Igor Illyn and Leonid Melodinsky were more prickly and suspicious. They warmed up as the job progressed, and in their own way, were as helpful as they could be. Needless to say, they soon became the ship's chess champions. Our explosives expert, Dr. Sydney Alford, kept to himself, but gradually began to fraternise and soon became the ship's undisputed scrabble champion. The *Sunday Times* photographers Paul Berrif and Ian Yeomans behaved very professionally, although Penrose was a pain in the arse to all concerned.

The *Stephaniturm's* diving system comprised two large chambers in which the divers slept and lived, complete with a shower and toilet compartment. There was an additional compartment that could be used to pressure down additional divers to join the others, or to decompress some divers while the others kept working. The toilet wastes from the pressure chamber were piped into a storage cylinder at a lower pressure and from there over the side of the ship. The toilet bowl was perforated all around under the rim. This was standard industry practice since a large American diver had his posterior seal the pan when the surface crew had discharged the holding tank and he was disemboweled. Amazingly, he survived

after emergency surgery under pressure in the chamber. It's called learning the hard way.

The diving bell locked onto the end compartment of one of the chambers. here the divers stored their suits and dressed and undressed for the dive. The bell was kept at the same internal pressure as the chambers. When maintenance was required in the bell, it had to be depressurised to atmospheric pressure. The problem was that it was full of heliox (helium and oxygen mixture) with only 3% of oxygen. That will not support life at the surface (another lesson the industry had learned the hard way). It was necessary to flush the bell out with 80/20 heliox before a surface mechanic could safely enter it.

For the *Edinburgh* dives, the storage depth in the chambers was to be 230 metres (750 feet). Every time the divers went down in the bell, they were pressurised the rest of the way to seabed depth and back up to 230 metres on the return to the chambers. This did not require any decompression and had the advantage of giving the divers a shorter final decompression at the end of the dive.

When the divers entered the bell to make a dive, the bell was sealed at a depth of 230 metres and unclamped from the chamber. It was then suspended over the "moonpool" (a rectangular hole down through the bottom of

The diving bell control panel. (Photo by M. Stewart)

the ship). There were rails running down the sides of the moonpool and in them ran a heavily weighted cage called a "cursor." The bell was first lifted snugly up into the cursor and then the cursor was lowered with the bell to push the bell through the heaving waters near the surface. At the bottom of the moonpool rails, the cursor stopped and the bell continued down under its own weight. Recovery of the bell was done the same way, in reverse, the cursor catching the bell and guiding it through the sea/air interface.

One of the greatest technical challenges on this trip was to keep the divers warm. The same problems of hypothermia that threatened the crews on the Arctic convoys threatened the divers. We expected a water temperature on the bottom of about 2C (36° F) (sea water freezes at about -4C). The normal heating system used for divers in the North Sea is to pump hot water down to them, which is then distributed around their rubber diving suits by a series of small perforated rubber pipes. These are designed to distribute the hot water in preference to the areas of the body that lose heat fastest; the head, hands, feet, neck, and the small of the back. Where the hot water enters at the front of the suit there is an inlet for cold water and a mixer valve so that the diver can adjust the temperature that he requires. We faced a serious difficulty to generate enough heat on the surface with our oil-fired boilers to overcome the heat losses in the bell umbilical so that the water would be hot enough to heat the diving bell, and still get through the diver's umbilical with enough heat to keep the diver warm.

We also had the problem of heating the divers' breathing gas. Unfortunately, helium is a very efficient conductor of heat. Coupled with the fact that, when spread out, human lungs cover the area of a football field, this means, however much external heat you apply, the diver would still die from hypothermia unless his breathing gas is heated. We solved this by channeling the gas through a small heat exchanger on the diver's back that was connected to the flow of hot water going to his suit.

The *Stephaniturm* was equipped with a full dynamic positioning (DP) system to hold the vessel on location without the use of anchors. This was critical to the success of the operation as we would not have been able to hold the vessel on anchors in such deep water. The primary system was deployed over an "A" frame at the stern of the vessel and consisted of a thin stainless steel wire lowered to the seabed with a weight. It was kept under tension with a winch and a computer was used to measure the angle of the wire when it was not exactly vertical. The computer then commanded the ship's thrusters to move the vessel so that the wire was vertical. There were also taut-wire systems to port and starboard, and there was a back-up system with which the computer could fix its position in relation to three acoustic transponders laid out on the seabed around the wreck. The great advantage of a DP system is that you can always head the vessel into any bad weather without actually moving position. This was very much the early days of DP systems and we all dreaded the "run off" where a system failure would produce an unplanned and abrupt move of the vessel with catastrophic consequences. When a diver was in the wreck, attached only by his fragile umbilical to the diving bell, it would only take a very small movement of the ship to rupture the umbilical and leave him to a certain death. The divers carried an emergency bailout bottle of gas, but at that depth it would only give them about three breaths, not even enough to get out of the wreck.

Mike O'Meara had two shift superintendents, who each ran a twelve-hour diving shift. The night shift was run by Derrick Hesketh, known as "Cyclops" after losing an eye in an accident. Dave Keene ran the day shift. Under each of them was a shift of life-support technicians whose non-stop job it was to monitor and control the atmosphere in the living chambers, to provide hot food and drinks on request, clean bed linen, piped music, and the other essentials of life. These were passed through a medical lock that could be opened from inside or outside the chamber once the pressure in it had been correctly adjusted. There was a persistent problem with providing hot food and drink; the act of compressing them to chamber pressure cooled them dramatically. Despite using polystyrene containers this problem has never really been solved, and is one of the regular complaints of divers. The life-support technicians also looked after the supply of gas to the divers in the diving bell. The shift supervisor could talk to the bellman (the diver who stayed in the bell), the diver in the water and to the divers in the living chambers.

The density of helium under pressure causes the vocal cords to vibrate differently than in air. This produces a "Donald Duck" effect, distorting the speech. After a few hours in the chamber, the divers could understand each other, but the surface crew needed an electronic unscrambler to make the divers intelligible.

All the bell handling and deck work was done by the deck crew under the deck supervisor, Ted Setchell, who reported to the shift supervisor.

The real stars of the show were the 12 divers who would put their lives on the line to make everyone's dream come true. These included:

Jim Tucker from South Africa
Pete Croft from New Zealand
Keith Cooper, known as "Scouse" Cooper
Brian Cutler
"Banjo" West, so called for his entertaining skills
Geoff Ruedavey from Australia
John Rossier from Rhodesia
"Legs" Diamond
Dougie Mathison
Pete Summers from South Africa
Dave Hardy from New Zealand
Eddie Wilde

Six of the divers were British and the rest were from Australia, New Zealand, and Rhodesia. Some of the best in the world had volunteered and now all our futures would depend on their courage and ability.

On September 2, the first eight divers entered the saturation chambers. Dressed universally in tee shirts and shorts, they carried personal effects, books, and fruit. By 2W standing order, they were all searched. This rather belittling procedure had become routine since we had once caught a diver going into saturation with a thick hard back book. This was found to have been hollowed out to contain a quarter bottle of whisky! Alcohol, drugs, and diving just don't mix. Needless to say, it was an insult to the intelligence of this professional crew, and gave rise to a number of unseemly offers to have all their body cavities inspected, but only by the ship's nurse.

Underlying the humorous banter was serious nervousness. They were about to be shut in, some for more than 40 days. The months of bravado in the bars was now replaced by the cold light of dawn. From now on their lives would be in the hands of their colleagues, and the myriad of complex mechanical systems on the *Stephaniturm*. As they entered the chambers, Keith Jessop was there to personally shake hands with each of them and wish them luck.

When divers are pressurised into saturation, the pressurisation has to take place slowly to avoid suppressing the Beta waves of the brain. This literally gives the diver the feeling of being squashed and can affect his working efficiency for several days. Mike O'Meara

had therefore planned to stop the divers at 152 meters (500 feet) for six hours of acclimatisation before continuing to the storage depth of 228 metres (750 feet). They then need time to acclimatise at the storage depth before going out to work.

Now in their steel home they were physically less than one inch from the familiar outside world, but it would take them a week to decompress to get out of the chambers, and it would take a doctor several hours to get into them, after he had reached the ship. They were now on their own, a tight-knit community relying on each others paramedical skills. Needless to say, if you suffer from claustrophobia, you don't become a diver. You have to be tolerant. In that closed environment, if one of the team sniffs, twitches, or farts too often, the others will end up killing him before the job is over.

The divers would all have been privately remembering the fate of *Stephaniturm*'s smaller sister ship that had sunk in a storm off Mexico with six divers in saturation. Nothing could be done to rescue them, and no one knows how long they stayed alive until their gas supply was exhausted.

The industry was learning these lessons and the *Stephaniturm* had a state-of-the-art rescue chamber. If the ship needed to be abandoned, the entire crew could collect in one of the saturation chambers which, together with its life support systems, could be launched over the side to enable the divers to be picked up and decompressed on another vessel. This was a great theory in the North Sea where other diving operations abounded, but we all knew that it was useless in the cold, isolated waters of the Arctic. Modern diver rescue systems are now incorporated in fireproof, self-propelled lifeboats in which the life support technicians can monitor and control the decompression in a safe environment.

I was particularly nervous about this aspect of the operation. We knew that polar lows could arrive in that area with violent seas with only a few hours' notice and, even in this day and age, big modern ships do sink. During my time at Comex, I had a team of divers working on a drilling ship off Nigeria. They were "bounce" diving in the days before saturation. They went down the same way to work out of the diving bell and then back up and locked onto the decompression chamber on deck, where they decompressed in relative comfort.

One day they had just finished a dive. Two divers were in the chamber decompressing when the rig drilled into a shallow gas pocket and found itself in the middle of a gas blowout. The gas aerated the water and the drill ship sank to the gunwhales. Everyone abandoned ship except the diving superintendent, who would not leave his divers. He transferred them back into the diving bell, attached a heavy tow line to it and unbolted the bell lift wire and umbilical. He then called up a supply boat on his hand-held radio and, between bursts of escaping gas he managed to throw them the tow line. They dragged the bell off the drill ship and pulled it clear of the gas blowout. He was then faced with the problem of saving himself. He ran to the bow of the drill ship and jumped off just as another pocket of gas erupted. Without buoyancy he sank like a stone and was brought up short by a fishing hook, left hanging off the bow by one of the crew. The hook caught in his arm and he managed to pull himself up the fishing line to the surface; then, in a gap between gas blows he was able to swim to a rescue vessel.

He had himself transferred to the supply boat which, fortunately, had a set of scuba diving equipment on board. He immediately went down to check that the divers were alive and started an emergency decompression of one metre per hour from memory. They set sail slowly for Port Harcourt some 24 hours away with a stop every hour to check on the divers and continue the decompression. After 12 hours they met up with a supply boat that had a crane and a diving compressor. He managed to get the bell lifted onto the deck and continued the journey to Port Harcourt. By now the divers were suffering from severe dehydration but were still twelve hours from completing the decompression. Ever resourceful, the superintendent took the valve out of a scuba tank, half filled the tank with water, refitted the valve and repressurised the tank. He then connected it up to the divers emergency breathing circuit on the bell and they were able to breathe moist air and keep themselves alive.

Twelve hours later they arrived in Port Harcourt where the bell was craned ashore and the decompression completed. Two very relieved divers emerged, slightly bruised and a lot lighter. Needless to say, I put the Superintendent forward for a Humane Society award, which was richly deserved and duly granted.

This was the sort of ability and resourcefulness for which the *Edinburgh* divers had been chosen. On the morning of September 3, the *Stephaniturm* arrived on location and Andy North from Racal Decca set about reactivating the three underwater Aquafix beacons that they had left behind when *Dammtor* had located the wreck in the spring. Concern mounted as two of the beacons failed to activate, but fortunately the third one worked perfectly and the *Edinburgh* was relocated. Ronnie Goetz immediately deployed the *Stephaniturm's* taut-wire system and established the vessel on DP. The back-up acoustic beacons would be placed later by the divers.

Early on the morning of Friday, September 4. an underwater TV system, capable of panning sideways and up and down, was lowered to the wreck and soon black and white images of the wreck were being seen flickering on TV monitors in the control room and other monitors to allow the ship's crew to see the action without disturbing the dive controllers. Once the job got underway, the divers would be using a new underwater colour camera they could take into the wreck with them to film the operation at close hand.

For the first dive, it was decided to try putting three divers in the bell; Banjo West, Legs Diamond, and Brian Cutler. This would allow two to work on the wreck and speed up work dramatically. This operation proved to be a disaster. The *Stephaniturm's* bell was just too small for three divers with their extra long umbilicals for working in the wreck. They suffered a severe build up of carbon dioxide in the bell and had to beat a hasty retreat before the divers passed out. Not a very auspicious start!

Reluctantly, we had to revert to a two-diver operation which would slow us down considerably. This way one diver would go out for four hours working on his own while the other handled the bell end of his umbilical and acted as emergency rescue diver in case the first diver got into difficulties. After four hours, they would change over and the

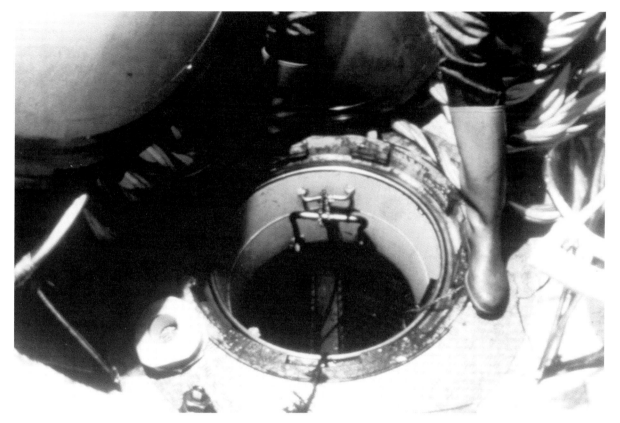

The lower hatch of the bell for the divers to get in and out. (Photo by M. Stewart)

bellman would go out for four hours. After eight hours the bell would be brought to the surface and the divers changed for two fresh ones. The first two divers would then have 16 hours to eat and rest before returning to duty again. In this way, apart from the time taken to raise and lower the bell, we could nominally keep one diver at work on the wreck 24 hours a day.

Each diver needed continual support from the surface to supply him with cutting equipment, tools, lifting wires, lights, cameras, and lifting baskets. These would be organised with the deck superintendent and required very careful liaison to ensure that items were never raised or lowered while the divers were out of the bell below them. It took some hours to analyse the reasons for the incident on the first dive and to double check all the equipment.

It was late afternoon when Pete Summers and Geoff Ruedavey entered the bell and made the long trip to the seabed. After the problems of the first dive, they were in a heightened state of awareness. It fell to Geoff to be the first man onto the wreck. As he pulled open the bell's bottom door and dropped below the bell, he stopped in awe. Nothing could have prepared him for the sight of this enormous ship lying so intact on the seabed in the glow of the diving bells lights. He was so mesmerized that, unplanned, he observed a two-minute silence in memory of the men who had gone to the bottom with her.

Geoff's first job was to position the acoustic beacons for ship's DP system to act as an automatic back-up in case the taut wire system failed. When this was completed, it was time for Pete Summers to make his dive. He gingerly started a preliminary inspection of the torpedo hole. The video taken by the "Scorpio" in the spring had shown a black hole with no detail of what lay beyond. Both Mike Stewart and Mike O'Meara needed to know whether we could get an easy route to bomb room this way, or whether we would need to laboriously cut through the hull again above the bomb room. The investigation had to be carefully executed. We did

not want dangerous debris in the pathway in the torpedo hole. It would also be the first time that one of the divers put his life in the hands of the DP system and entered a hole with a jagged edge that could sever his connection with this world in an instant if the *Stephaniturm's* DP system failed. Pete had seen some ammunition boxes in the torpedo hole and this was verified with the pan and tilt video camera.

It was perhaps not surprising that, with all the stresses of the first dive, the

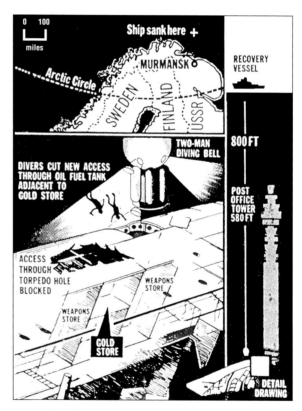

A graphic illustrating the position of the HMS Edinburgh.

divers did not use the gas recovery system. This wasted a lot of gas and brought them a swift rebuke from Don Rodocker. On future dives the new system would have to be used systematically or the gas stocks on the *Stephaniturm* would not last.

The diving now settled into a routine and the next two bell runs produced a serious inspection of the torpedo hole with disappointing results. The bad news was that the fuel tank was completely clogged with large debris that would need lifting equipment to shift them. This would have to be done with direct access from above, so we were already to plan "B" with a new hole to cut above the bomb room. The divers could see there was no gas build-up in the fuel tank, so normal oxyarc cutting gear could be used.

On deck all this seemed painfully slow. The Soviet representatives and David Keogh were starting to complain about the cramped viewing facilities and lack of action. It took them a long time to realise that diving is a slow business, and that watching divers in real time is like watching grass grow. Mike Stewart made it politely, but abundantly clear that he was not going to be hurried and that had better get used to it. We were already beginning to suffer from Malcolm's great fear of more watchers than doers.

During the next two dives, Mike Stewart meticulously checked and rechecked his measurements along the hull from the torpedo hole to ensure that the cut into the hull would be directly above the bomb room. He had calculated that we could cut just below the bottom of the armour plating. That would save us some very difficult cutting and a lot of time.

When work started on cutting through the hull it went very smoothly until

HMS Edinburgh *hull plating being lifted on board. (Photo by J. Clarke)*

Pete Summers had a minor blow back of the oxygen that gave him a thump in the chest and broke his welding visor. This is a hazard of underwater cutting and highlighted our caution in bringing shaped trepanning charges with us.

The next issue of the *Sunday Times* showed Barry Penrose in his true colours and just about put Malcolm into orbit. It was a lurid sensational article about carbon dioxide problems in the bell and the blow back Pete Summers had suffered. It threw our insurers into shock and caused us massive problems. It is hard to believe that journalists can be so negative to achieve sensation when presented with a ringside seat at the most exiting salvage of the century. Warning messages were sent to the ship that any more negative reporting would result in a ban of all communications from the vessel.

Wreckage being lifted on board. (Photo by J. Clarke)

When the divers completed the cut through the hull, the plating was lifted clear to expose the mass of debris in the fuel tank. This had been caused because the transverse bulkhead at frame 93, the stern of the bomb room, was also the stern end of the fuel tank. When the torpedo hit, the debris from the machinery room had fallen into the fuel tank along with debris from the small arms magazine and the store room. These had lain in the bottom of the fuel tank during the final engagement. As the vessel sank stern first all this debris had accumulated at the stern end of the fuel tank — frame 93.

It was a daunting task, but there was no alternative but to remove the debris by hand. Some of this was easy and was put into skips by hand, other pieces had to be slung and craned out. One in particular was an eight-ton compressor unit that had to be lifted out with the ship's crane and dumped on the seabed. This was exhausting work for the divers, but in a way prepared them for the work ahead in clearing the bomb room.

One of the major problems was visibility. When a new shift of divers arrived in the wreck, the water would be gin clear

Naval message from HMS Edinburgh.
(Photo by R. Wharton)

and they could survey and film clearly. As soon as they started to move their feet and move debris they were enveloped in clouds of swirling silt, and from then on would have to do all their work by feel. This frustrated observers on the surface; for long periods there would be nothing for them to see. A water lift was soon rigged using the ship's 4-inch fire main which helped clear the visibility around the diver if he stopped work for a few minutes.

It was at this stage of the operation that the dreaded Pio struck, hitting

A blank message form from the HMS Edinburgh.
(Photo by R. Wharton)

Banjo West, Legs Diamond, and Brian Cutler first. These divers were decompressed for treatment and John Rossier and Dougie Mathison pressured up to join the team.

By now the debris being removed from the fuel tank revealed live shells, fuses, and pom-pom ammunition. Samples of these were brought to the surface for examination by both Mikes and Dr. Alford to report on their condition and stability. The divers were now starting to find nostalgic items from the store room, including a very well preserved tin of Brasso and numerous pads of Naval message forms which regularly blocked the water lift. Although these were of paper, they had survived 39 years of immersion. Sydney Alford took on the painstaking task of restoring these message forms, which he then handed out as souvenirs. The divers also recovered a fork with the markings of the German Third Reich. To this day, we have no idea how it got there.

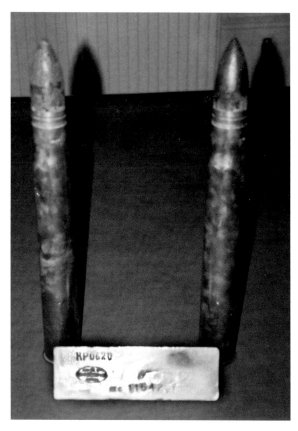

Two "Three Pounder" shells and an ingot from HMS *Edinburgh. (Photo by R. Wharton)*

As the divers worked their way down to the bulkhead of the bomb room, they found a wide split in it caused by the torpedo explosion. This was a mixed blessing. On the positive side, it meant that we knew what was behind the bulkhead and would not need to use our trepanning charge to cut through it. Unfortunately, the breach in the bulkhead meant that the bomb room had also filled up with

Bofars shell case and bomb fuse plugs from HMS Edinburgh. *(Photo by R. Wharton)*

silt and debris. Keith Cooper was the first to get a good look in through the split and reported that it looked like a disused cellar three-quarters full of silt and rubbish, comprised of various sizes of bombs with large numbers of bomb fuses, boxes of fuses, bomb trolleys, broken pipes, cabling, broken ducting, twisted bomb racks, and paravane wires. There was also material washed in from the store room forward, including more Naval message pads. Of course, under all that lay the 93 wooden boxes that we had come all this way to find. It appeared that the bomb room was intact, but emptying it was going to prove a formidable task.

Back in Aberdeen, Malcolm and I were getting seriously worried. It was more than two weeks since the *Stephaniturm* had sailed. Far from getting the long awaited "Dog 36" code over the radio, we could sense the anxiety in Mike Stewart's voice. He knew what this meant to us financially. His daily reports include lists of additional supplies he required. It was clear the Pio was becoming serious and we would have to send up the company doctor, Mike Childs. More seriously, with all the extra clearance work to do, we would need more gas. Reluctantly, we made plans to charter a supply boat to make the long trip to the Barents Sea. This was to cost some £75,000, and the only people to pay for that were Malcolm and I. It did not come under anyone else's no cure, no pay deal. Our

daily worry was the weather. We had already had a couple of short sharp storms that had shut us down, and it was now getting very late in the year. With so much work left do we had visions of having to abandon the site until the next spring, with all the attendant risks of piracy in our absence.

Our chief worry, though, was the money. We owned 2W and could afford to pay ourselves well, but we did not have substantial cash assets. The exposure that we had undertaken on this project was now more than the company alone could afford. If we failed, the castle that Jackie and I had so lovingly restored and Malcolm's farm would have to go. It was a gloomy time. The carbon dioxide incident on the first dive reminded us by how fragile a thread our futures hung. Any serious diving accident or mechanical failure would shut us down. As those bleak days dragged on, we were also adopting a very low public profile with no discussion at all of Operation Greyhound. Our worry after the irrational reporting in the *Sunday Times* became even harder to bear.

Then, to add insult to injury, came Penrose's most stupid act of all. Despite giving instructions that no more press releases were to be sent from *Stephaniturm* we were horrified to open our *Sunday Times* and find lurid headlines alleging that the divers had lined up skulls with lights in them to frighten other divers from going into the wreck. When we came down out of orbit and called the ship, we found out what had happened. Penrose, who was already being ostracized by just about everyone on board, had grabbed one of the divers (who had already been warned about him) coming out of saturation and asked him what it was like down there. "Christ," said the diver, "fucking awful, they've got skulls lined up with lights in them and bones everywhere, fucking terrifying mate." Needless to say, he took the typical diver's humour as fact and called the *Sunday Times* with the "story" without bothering to confirm it with anyone else on board. We were not allowing him access to the control room, but the MoD and Soviet representatives were there all the time and every aspect of the operation was filmed all the time. Had anything remotely like that happened the MoD representative David Keogh would have shut us down immediately. During the whole operation, the divers found only animal bones, which were probably from the cold room food store nearby.

For Malcolm and I, as well as Mike Stewart and John Clarke, this was the last straw. We pulled the plug on Penrose once and for all with no further communication from him allowed to leave the ship. It is not hard to imagine how frustrated a journalist becomes when cut off from his paper and his public. He made efforts to persuade the ship's radio officer to send out messages for him, with offers of financial inducements, but to no avail. Bottled up on the ship he was to turn his anger toward Keith Jessop with far reaching consequences.

Meanwhile, the two Mike's continued professionally to overcome the difficulties when they arose. They were well assisted by John Clarke, who was trying to prevent Penrose from sending out any more inflammatory and incorrect reports, and trying to keep the Soviets out of Mike's hair. The divers, using cutting equipment, enlarged the split in the bomb room bulkhead to make an opening big enough to enable them to clear the room. They then laboriously loaded the debris into a skip for removal. As soon as this work started, they lost all visibility and either had to work by touch alone or wait for the water lift to improve visibility. There was a moment of intense excitement when part of a wooden box was brought to the surface with stencilling on it. This was urgently checked against the information that we had been given by the Soviets, only to be told by Dr. Alford that it was part of a box of fuses.

Now Keith Cooper went down with bad Pio and Dougie Mathison suffered some bad hot water burns to the ankles. He had become too cold and turned up the heat at his hot water control valve. Unfortunately, this coincided with the diver in the bell turning off the

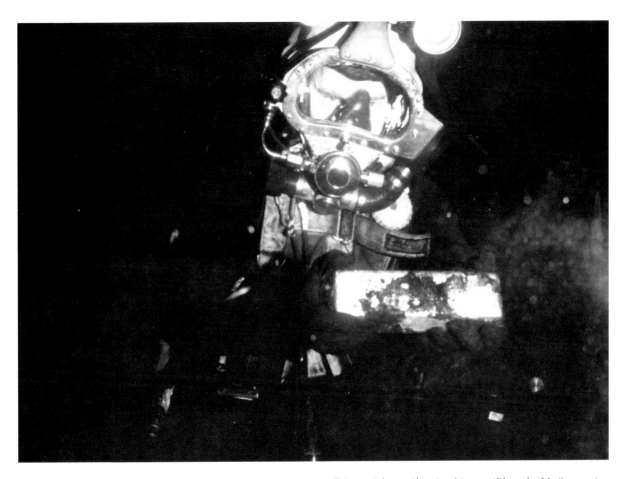

Diver with an oil-stained ingot. (Photo by M. Stewart)

bell heater. As this normally took about 4 degrees from the incoming water temperature it had the effect of increasing the temperature by 4 degrees just as Dougie turned up the heat. This left him with badly scalded ankles. In addition to these problems, the divers were all starting to show signs of fatigue. Mike O'Meara was planning to put Banjo West, Legs Diamond, and Brian Cutler back into saturation as soon as their ears were fully recovered.

It was now Wednesday, September 16, and the divers' work was beginning to show some results. Hopes soared when the divers reported that they could see boxes in the debris. On dive 27 at 10:48 p.m., John Rossier suddenly screamed "I've found the Gold!

I've found the Gold! I've found the Gold!" This was exactly four months to the day since the *Dammtor* had located the *Edinburgh.*

His high-pitched scream frightened the shift supervisor Dave Keene half to death. Screams from divers are usually very bad news.

In clouds of thick silt, John Rossier had been heaving debris into a skip by feel when he suddenly felt a piece heavier than normal. He lifted up until it was touching his face plate and through the murky water saw that unmistakable glint of gold. He could clearly see the Hammer and Sickle stamped in an oval cartouche and the bar's serial number KP 0620.

Euphoria spread through the ship, the bar was carefully placed in a cage and lifted to the surface. It was passed to Keith for the well-deserved honour of carrying around the ship, including locking it into the saturation chambers so that the divers could feel the results of their efforts. Keith was understandably emotionally attached to this bar and actually paid the VAT and kept it as a souvenir.

That night Jackie and I were at a dinner party with friends in Kincardinshire, some miles south of Aberdeen. Malcolm and I took turns receiving Mike Stewart's nightly radio calls from the ship and this was his night. I had given

him the phone number where he could contact me if he got any news. That night I remember we were almost finished with dinner, when I was called to the phone in the kitchen. My heart in my mouth, standing amongst the mundane debris of an excellent meal, I took the phone. It was Malcolm's wife Marion and all she said was "Dog 36." I went cold and all I could say was "Thank God, we're saved."

When I recovered my composure and returned to the table Jackie, sitting opposite me, did not look up from her conversation with the guest next to her. I finally got her attention and said "We've got a Dog 36!" "Oh," she said and turned back to her neighbour and continued "Yes we've got four children, two boys and two girls and———"

I was mortified at her lack of reaction to such fantastic news that would change our lives. But upon reflection it probably did not make such an impact on her as I had not burdened her with the knowledge that I had put her home on the line!

Mike Stewart's first thought amid the excitement on board was to call us and put us out of our misery of waiting. Although the main line of communication from the ship was back to 2W, David Bona was desperate to try and stay in the loop and use his

An ingot straight from the sea. (Photo by M. Stewart)

The Soviet representative Igor Illyn on board the
Stephaniturm *on location. (Photo by J. Clarke)*

comical codes. He wanted to act as interface to pass on messages from David Keogh to the Salvage Association on the status of cargo recovered. Sometime after midnight that night, when the ship was beginning to return to its normal routine, David Keogh called the night number that Bona had given him to pass on the news. To his surprise, over the crackly radio link he heard Kennelmaid answer the phone,

Bona's secretary Brenda. She was clearly taking her responsibilities very seriously.

"Who is speaking?" asked Kennelmaid.

"This is Henry here speaking from *Stephaniturm*," and heard her say to Bona, "Its David Keogh for you." Keogh then said "Is that Kennel?"

"Yes" said Bona.

"Kennel this is Keeper," said Keogh. "Operation Greyhound, Dog 36 zero one Collar, Over." After the first bar Greek numbers were used after the Dog 36 to indicate how many bars had been recovered.

For Malcolm and I we had crossed the Rubicon. We knew that if one bar was there, all or most of the others would be and we now needed good luck and good weather to complete the job. On board *Stephaniturm* the atmosphere was electric. They had all reached the same conclusion and just wanted to get on with the recovery work. Even the Soviets began to smile and Penrose was allowed to send a censored report back to the *Sunday Times*.

A sack of gold ingots being lifted aboard. (Photo by J. Clarke)

Keogh, Illyn, and Melodinsky all now had something do. A burgeoning bureaucracy was to develop around the gold bars. Each had to be cleaned, its serial number recorded, along with its original weight that was also stamped on it. Each bar had to be photographed three times by Ian Yeomans and signed for by the three representatives, David Keogh for the UK, Igor Illyn for the Soviet Union, and Keith Jessop on behalf of the Salvors. How they loved it. It kept them happy for hours. At the end each session, with Fagin-like glee, they would put their individual locks on the paint store that now served as the new bullion room.

Soon the divers were finding bars in large numbers. In one dive alone Dougie Mathison brought up 40 bars worth four million pounds. On shore, Malcolm and I waited with baited breath each night for Mike Stewart's call and the latest tally. A few days after our first "Dog 36," I was hosting a major dinner party for clients of 2W at the castle. It was my turn on radio watch. Mike called in while we were all at dinner, I could tell by his voice that he was excited. This was the actual day of Dougie's big haul.

"I have a new Dog 36 for you," said Mike, "its Sigma Epsilon."

I reached for my briefcase and suddenly realised that I had left my code book in the office.

"I've left my bloody code book in the office Mike, can you give me a clue?"

There was a short pause and Mike came back and said, "Well, it's a popular French position in bed."

I don't know which pleased the dinner guests more that night, the tally of 69 bars or the way we decoded it.

As the job progressed, our children became fascinated with the number count of the bars. The intercom system in the castle has always been to shout up one of the spiral staircases. After each call whoever was in the kitchen would rush to the bottom of the stairs shouting "New Dog 36, eighty seven!" They were exciting times.

Tastes good! (Photo by M. Stewart)

OUR SHIP

COMES IN

CHAPTER 7

By this time, the Soviets had positioned two Auxiliary Information Gathering ships (spy vessels) alongside the *Stephaniturm*. One was keeping far too close to the *Stephaniturm*'s stern and ignored Captain Goetz's pleas to keep further away for fear of interfering with the *Stephaniturm*'s DP system. The Soviet Air Force was regularly overflying the *Stephaniturm* and the atmosphere was becoming more oppressive. Illyn and Melodinsky were creating a scene because they expected to get a colour photo of each bar recovered delivered to them on board. They were being photographed in accordance with the contract, but the *Stephaniturm* did not have a dark room to process the film. This stupid wrangle was eventually resolved, but was typical of the pedantic behaviour of the Soviets throughout the operation.

As the initial euphoria wore off, the task of emptying the bomb room

The crowded deck of the Stephaniturm *prior to sailing. (Photo by J. Clarke)*

became an increasingly tiring job for the divers, who were beginning to show serious signs of fatigue. The ear infections were starting to take their toll on the weakened divers and we were forced to send our company doctor, Mike Childs, out to the ship. He made an arduous journey by air and sea and arrived in a very seasick state to minister to the divers. Dougie Mathison had fallen in the bell trunking and dislocated his shoulder. The Doctor had to strap this, treat his scalded ankles, and treat him for the Pio ear infection.

As the work dragged on slowly removing debris from the bomb room by hand it was becoming increasingly apparent that we would not be able to finish the job without putting the divers at serious risk. Twice during this period the ship was driven off station by sudden storms and valuable time was lost. We really were at the end of the season and would have to give up. On October 7, with 431 of the 465 bars on board the *Stephaniturm*, Mike O'Meara and Mike Stewart called Malcolm Williams and said that we must cease operations. Malcolm and I agreed immediately.

Against all odds we had achieved the impossible. We had recovered 93% of the *Edinburgh*'s cargo from a record depth in the most hostile waters in the world, and we had done it without any serious injury. We were only too glad to stop while we were ahead. The weather had blown up again and Mike O'Meara told us that the divers had five bars in the canvas lined steel mesh bag ready to lift on the next dive. Despite that we all agreed that we would not push our luck, it was time to go.

David Keogh, as the ship's padre, called all the crew together for a Service of Remembrance on the *Stephaniturm*'s deck. Keith Cooper was chosen to cast the wreath onto the water to honour the 57 officers and men who had gone down with their ship on this spot 39 years ago, after a gallant struggle to save the ship and its precious cargo. The long decompression of the divers began and the ship headed for Murmansk to hand the Soviets their share of our efforts. An effervescent Keith was already calling home to order his new Porsche which would be waiting on the quay side for him when the ship finally got back to Peterhead.

Late the next day, the *Stephaniturm* nosed into its allocated berth in Murmansk and tied up. The berth had been chosen alongside a railway siding where the Soviets had a special carriage waiting that was to return the gold to the vaults in Moscow. Under the watchful eyes of many armed guards a large delegation of Soviet officials boarded the vessel. After much hand-shaking and congratulation they were led to the *Stephaniturm*'s new bullion room, that only a few weeks before had been a bosuns locker. In a modern day "ceremony of the keys' Igor Illyn, David

Keogh, and Keith Jessop for the salvors stepped forward with their keys to open their individual locks. As the Soviets tried unsuccessfully to open their lock derisive laughter broke out from the assembled divers and crew. The Soviets, emulating Queen Victoria, were not amused. As their embarrassed efforts continued to open the door the atmosphere became more and more tense, accompanied by the ominous sound of Kalashnikov semi-automatic rifles being cocked. The divers had squirted glue in the locks overnight, and were by now convulsed with laughter. At this point the Soviet delegation suffered a serious sense of humour failure and hacksaws had to be fetched to laboriously saw off the locks.

Fortunately, when the door finally swung open, the sight of so much gold in serried ranks on the shelves of the paint store evaporated the Soviet's anger and good old fashioned gold fever took over. There now followed a laborious physical split of the gold under the mutually suspicious eyes of everybody. First, the gold was split into thirds. This entailed a detailed recording of bar numbers and weights. At this stage we had to use the weights that were stamped on the bars, even though many bars were scratched and would no longer be that exact weight. The gold market describes an ingot as being "of good delivery" if its physical weight is exactly the weight stamped upon it.

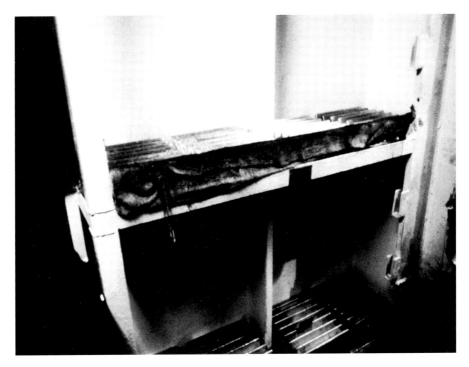

Above, the converted paint store on the Stephaniturm. *(Photo by M. Stewart)*
Below, in the paint locker, more than £8 million in this picture alone. (Photo by M. Stewart)

When an ingot is not of good delivery, it usually ends up being sold as gold for industrial use, rather than being kept as bullion.

The two governments had agreed that the bars would not be cut, and that the split would be to the nearest bar in the Soviet's favour, with the Soviets to subsequently make a cash adjustment to the British Government. The Soviet share of the gold was now split 55% to them and 45% to the salvors, again to the nearest bar in favour of the Soviets with a cash adjustment to follow. The same split was now carried out with the British share of the gold. Once again the split was to the nearest bar in favour of the British Government with a cash adjustment to follow. In view of what subsequently happened, it still rankles me that the salvor should have been so badly treated in always having to take a lesser share and then wait indefinitely for the contractual cash adjustment. After all, we had carried out the salvage and the two governments had contributed absolutely nothing.

The Russian team leaving the Stephaniturm *at Murmansk. John Clarke and Mike Stewart at the top of the steps shortly after the "Super Glue" incident. (Photo by J. Clarke)*

Once the main division of bullion had been carried out, the salvor's share was subdivided between 2W, JMRL, OSA, and Racal Decca in accordance with their shares, 37.12% to 2W, 10% to JMRL, 50.4% to OSA and 2.48% to Racal Decca. This was again split to the nearest bar and was subsequently adjusted in cash without argument, as at least the salvors were all on the same side. We were now able to formally transfer our individual holdings to our London bullion dealer to ensure that it was in their ownership at the time of importation into the UK. This was to ensure that the postponed accounting treatment would apply and we would not pay VAT at Peterhead.

The Soviet gold was now crated and loaded into the waiting railway carriage for its journey to Moscow. Once this was accomplished, the Soviets relaxed and actually organised a party for the crew in a local hotel where, to the amusement of the Soviets, the crew (somewhat the worse for vodka) proceeded to de-bag David Keogh.

In late September, the German government advised us, via OSA, that they had information that there was the possibility of a terrorist attack being launched against the *Stephaniturm*. While Malcolm and I were not too concerned about the gold, which was now well insured, we were extremely worried about any risk to the divers and the ship's crew. We requested a security meeting with the MoD as a matter of urgency. This was held at the Salvage Associations office in London on September 22. This was attended by all interested parties, including the MoD, the Department of Trade (Shipping Policy Division), the bank of England, and the Metropolitan Police. I asked if the government could provide a Naval vessel to escort the *Stephaniturm* back to Peterhead.

"Certainly," said the MoD, that will cost you £75,000 per day for a frigate.

"But," I said, "a great deal of the gold on board belongs to the British Government," to which the answer was "Yes, but you are the responsible contractor."

Needless to say, I protested and eventually they grudgingly offered to supply an armed detachment of Marine Commandos to travel back on the ship from Murmansk. I felt that this was a satisfactory solution and passed the information on to OSA.

At this point the German government got in on the act and said "Ja, very good idea, but ziz is a German schiffe und it vill be ze German Commandos." This opinion was passed back to the MoD and, as far as I know, the two governments were still arguing about whose troops they were going to use when the *Stephaniturm* arrived back at Peterhead, thankfully unscathed. Needless to say, this did not do a lot to improve my view of the British establishment. The divers and crew were blissfully unaware of this threat.

They were also blissfully unaware of the next threat that we, and they, faced, again from a very ungrateful British Establishment. I was sitting in my office in Aberdeen when the ever faithful Pat came into my office to tell me that there were two pinstriped gentlemen wishing to see me. They both had briefcases with E.R. embossed on them. I had seen enough of those to know who carried them and told Pat that I was too busy to see anyone without an appointment. They were more than a little insistent and refused to leave until they had seen me. By this time they had stated that they were from the Inland Revenue. I sat them down in my office and asked what I could do for them.

"We have come to collect the income tax on the diver's earnings," they said. I patiently pointed out to them that the divers, half of whom were foreign residents, were not employed by 2W, but were employed by a subcontractor who was contracted to us on a no cure, no pay basis. "Not good enough," they said, we are not leaving until you give us 50% of their earnings. Taking a deep breath, I patiently pointed out that they had not even left Murmansk yet, and I did not know what their earnings were.

All of this made no impression on them at all and they kindly offered to arrest me if I did not give them a cheque on the spot. The upshot of all this was that they forced me to give them a cheque for some £150,000. Again, all this was before we had received a penny. How was I to break this news to an incredibly brave group of men who were coming back, rightly expecting the adulations of a grateful country?

I felt that the very least we could do would be to give each of the divers a personal memento of this great achievement. I commissioned my older brother Joe who is a leading goldsmith, with my next brother Chris, to make an individual gold ingot on a gold chain for each diver.

On October 9, the *Stephaniturm* left Murmansk with the congratulations of the Soviets ringing in their ears and serious vodka hangovers ringing in their heads. As she sailed, I thought ruefully of the expropriation insurance that that Malcolm and I had bought from Lloyds at a cost of £70,000 to protect us against the risk of the Soviets confiscating our gold on some flimsy excuse while we were in their hands at Murmansk. It had turned out to be a very expensive waste of money, but faced with the same situation again, I would still buy the insurance.

There was a euphoric party atmosphere on board for the journey home. Unusual for an offshore support vessel, the drinks flowed and the week long party reached its crescendo when the main diving team finally finished their decompression on October 13, and emerged to the outside world, and a serious drink.

Malcolm and I only found out much later that, having come from Comex, the *Stephaniturm* was loaded with red wine. Alcohol is prohibited offshore in the North Sea for obvious safety reasons. Mike Stewart and John Clarke took it upon themselves to class the Barents Sea as "outside the North Sea" and red wine was served to the crew with each meal. Malcolm and I would have had a fit if we had known at the time. With hindsight, it did no harm and doubtless made a difficult job easier.

In the early hours of the October 16, the *Stephaniturm* eased into the port of Peterhead. A complete arm of the dock had been cleared for her and security was intense. Malcolm and I were waiting on the dock as she came in, standing alongside Keith's new Porsche. We had not had the heart to tell the team of the tax blow that the government had just dealt them, and decided to wait until we had presented each of them with their miniature ingots before breaking the news. As you can imagine, it really deflated them. As a result of this treatment I wrote a personal letter of complaint to Mrs. Thatcher and received a reply that was obviously written by the Treasury and signed by her. The letter was a complete brush off by the Civil Service who were now closing ranks.

Under the watchful and incredulous eyes of the Peterhead Police the gold was unloaded from the *Stephaniturm* into a waiting Brinksmat truck for the long journey to the Bank of England in London. There was an incredible security organisation surrounding this journey. The Brinksmat armoured truck had a large police escort for the entire journey, but because of the county organisation of police forces, the escort was changed at each county boundary, an amazingly inefficient system.

The Brinksmat bullion van waiting at Peterhead Harbour.
(Photo by J. Clarke)

Needless to say, we were being charged for this exceptional convoy and its escort.

During the welcoming ceremony at Peterhead, Barrie Penrose was nowhere to be seen, but there were urgent meetings behind closed doors between the MoD and the Salvage Association. That night I held a major welcoming party at the Castle, attended by all the key players, with the notable exception of the MoD and the Salvage Association who inexplicably declined to attend. Our visitors book for that day is headed "The Day our Ship Came In."

It later transpired that the reason that the MoD and the Salvage Association did not attend the party was that, in the clandestine meetings on the ship at Peterhead, Penrose had accused the Salvage Association of impropriety in letting the contract. It would appear that Penrose, being cut off from his public and heavily censored while on board the *Stephaniturm*, had focused his resentment on Keith Jessop and had accused him of bribing John Jackson at the Salvage Association to get the *Edinburgh* contract. This was a monstrously untrue and unfair allegation, as was subsequently proved but only after causing immense damage and cost to Keith Jessop.

As early as 1978, during a downturn in the offshore industry in the North Sea, we, along with other diving companies, had contacted the Salvage Association to try to get salvage contracts at a depth that we could carry out with divers. The main contact point at the Salvage Association's offices in London was John Jackson, the Senior Manager, although sometimes we would meet his boss Arthur Prince and Stan Holness of the Department of Trade. Both Jackson and Prince were concerned that, for many years, Risdon Beazley had enjoyed a virtual monopoly of the salvage contracts, and had been able to virtually dictate their terms. They actively encouraged several diving companies to bid for salvage work. In the case of the *Edinburgh*, the Shipping Policy Division of the Department of Trade and Industry (DOT) was heavily involved. It was their Mr. Brian Stambrey who wrote to us in August of 1980 to advise us that the DOT Shipping Policy Division had

decided that a blast and grab operation would not be acceptable and that they would only be considering a diving operation. We had felt certain that the government would prefer to use a British contractor rather than a Norwegian one. For one thing, they certainly would not have extorted £3,000,000 of VAT from a Norwegian company.

Penrose alleged that Jackson had favoured Keith Jessop in the award of the contract. Malcolm and I knew this could not be the case. It was my suggestion to bid at 45%. If Jessop had any kind of inside track he would have told me that we did not need to go that low. By the time the *Stephaniturm* returned to Peterhead, Keith Jessop had finally begun to realise what we had been telling him for months about Bona and Ringrose. When Bona pressed for the £100,000 for "charities" approved by Prince Charles, Keith began to smell a very large rat and promptly dispensed with both their services. Bona and Ringrose then found that Penrose had a very receptive shoulder to cry on and so fuelled the fires.

While this unseemly row was brewing, Malcolm and I were venturing into the dangerous waters of gold trading. We had our gold, as well as our subcontractor's, sitting in the London bullion market, awaiting our order to sell. The problem was that our subcontractors were all to be paid in cash and their deals were not in any way linked to the gold price. Throughout the salvage operation, the price of gold had been steadily rising and had just levelled off at around the £236 per ounce. This was the highest point in the market for a considerable time and the pundits were predicting that it would continue to rise. We soon learned the terminology of the market, and how the bullion dealers had a morning and afternoon fix each day to set the price.

After an exciting week of watching the price fluctuations we decided that we could no longer gamble with everyone else's money and should proceed to sell all the gold without further delay. I duly phoned our appointed bullion dealer and told our contact there that we had decided to sell all the gold now. This upper crust son of the gentry told me that this was a bit rash. He said that, to get the best out of the market, I should sell 20% of the gold a day over a five-day period. These were the experts, so I agreed and we sold 20% at £236 per ounce. The next day the price had fallen to £230 per ounce. After a somewhat frank phone call, my friendly neighbourhood bullion dealer said, "Don't worry, its just a fluctuation in the market, the price will be back up again tomorrow." Needless to say, the price drifted steadily down and three weeks later, in order to meet our commitments, we sold the balance of the gold at £208 per ounce.

Thanks to that excellent professional advice, which overcame our natural instincts, Malcolm and I personally lost £500,000. Needless to say, the Inland Revenue and Customs and Excise were not there to commiserate and offer assistance and tax relief for that loss. The only positive thing that I can say about our bullion dealer was that they arranged for 40 of the gold bars to be taken to Lloyds and, under high security, these were displayed in a glittering stack on the floor of the old underwriting room in front of the Lutine Bell. We arranged this to thank all the professionals at Lloyds who had backed us and shared the risk. The event certainly interrupted the underwriting business for a few hours.

We now set about paying all our subcontractors and investors for their share of the great reward. OSA had performed their part of the contract impeccably. Very thoughtfully, they cast a small number of gold coins from one of the bars and presented them to all the key participants. Racal Decca produced a beautiful paperweight with a replica gold bar cast inside it. From Project Manager Mike Stewart down, everyone concerned fulfilled their roles with the highest level of professionalism. The only sour note was struck by Penrose, who tried to create a scandal out of an historic, world-beating operation.

Having made his unfounded allegations against Keith Jessop and John Jackson, the ponderous British legal system creaked into life. Malcolm and I were astonished to be visited by the CID to take detailed statements from us about the salvage operation, which we duly gave. We told the police at the time that it was a complete farce and that I had decided the percentage at which the consortium would bid. Despite all that evidence, in August 1982 the police raided the homes of Jackson and Jessop at six in the morning and arrested them both and drove them to London for questioning. Both men had already given statements voluntarily and would have driven down to London for further questioning if so requested. This ridiculous overkill was to continue throughout this inexplicable witch hunt. By this time, Penrose had written a book, published by Grenada Publishing. Instead of being a first-hand account of the salvage of the century, the book was a bitter, and I suspect jealous, attack on Keith Jessop. Keith had by now hired a professional firm of lawyers in Leeds. They immediately moved to have the book withdrawn from circulation and sued for damages.

The case finally came to trial at the Old Bailey in March 1984. Surprisingly, Malcolm and I were called as witnesses for the prosecution, despite the fact that our statements made it very clear that we in no way agreed with the prosecution's case. The upshot of all this was that Jessop and Jackson were quickly acquitted and awarded full costs. Jessop went on to be awarded damages against Grenada Publishing and Barrie Penrose. While Jessop had the cash and the resilience to withstand this stressful ordeal, John Jackson was not so well equipped. He had no personal funds and was forced onto Legal Aid. To add to his misery, the Salvage Association suspended him and subsequently retired him, despite the definitive proof of his innocence.

In any other country in the world, the participants in such a world-beating operation would be lauded and rewarded. In the Britain of today, we did not even get a letter of thanks for the £8,000,000 that we gave to the treasury. What infuriated me even more was that, despite repeated efforts by Sir Maitland Mackie, the then Lord Lieutenant of Aberdeenshire, the divers received no recognition at all for their efforts. The only consolation I received was to hear, as a result of a Commons question, that the Governments share of the salvage money had been used to help fund the war in the Falklands. Sir Maitland Mackie was told by "the powers that be" that an award for the divers was not considered to be appropriate as they had been well paid for their efforts! What an attitude in a country where pop stars and captains of industry are forever receiving political-ly-motivated awards.

All this served to confirm my view that Britain is burdened by appalling civil servants who are more interested in their own awards and pensions than in the good of this country. What a different situation it would have been if it had been a French company that had carried out the salvage!

While Keith Jessop and John Jackson's personal ordeals were being played out, we were in regular contact with the Salvage Association and the DOT. We were trying to arrange for the balancing payments due to us from the British government and the Soviets for the exact share of the gold, as we had been underpaid on both accounts to avoid having to cut up any of the ingots. In addition to the balance due, there was a provision in the salvage contract for interest to be applied in the case of late payment. At this time, the Falklands had started and all our contacts in the Shipping Policy Division of the DOT became completely "unavailable," as they were responsible for chartering in the merchant ships that were to transport supplies to the South Atlantic. We maintained the pressure on the Salvage Association for payment, but with no success at all. The Salvage Association was the contracting party on behalf of the two governments and it was to them that we had to apply for payment. As the months and years dragged on, it became increasingly apparent that neither they, nor the British government had the balls to apply to the Soviets for the amount outstanding.

Never in all my years in business have I seen such a blatant breach of contract by supposedly honest and civilised governments. While we were claiming the rest of our payment from the first salvage, we were pushing for permission to return to the wreck. The world now knew that there were 34 ingots left on board the *Edinburgh*, worth some £3,500,000. We had, at great expense, cut the access hole and cleared most of the debris from the bomb room. It would now be a relatively easy task for someone to go back for the rest. We obviously had title to complete the job and considered that we "owned" the hole in the wreck.

We could understand a reluctance to let us return while Jessop's trial was underway, but as soon as he was vindicated, there was no excuse at all to prevent us from returning to finish the job. The next excuse was again the disruption caused by the Falklands war. As soon as that was over, we continued to push hard for the outstanding monies and for permission to return.

SAILING IN

OTHER WATERS

CHAPTER 8

During this drawn-out process that was to last for five years, until 1986, life had to go on. The 2W diving business was greatly boosted by out success with the *Edinburgh*. It was the talk of the industry and no one ever again questioned whether we were technically qualified for deep-diving contracts. We now had substantial funds and were able to indulge our more general salvage interests. While treasure is nice to have, I have always been fundamentally interested in archeology, particularly marine archeology. There are historically important wrecks like the *Victory* that will always fascinate me, even though there is no prospect of profit in them. Mike Stewart is of a similar inclination and together we decided to spend some of our funds on an investigation of the mysterious Spanish Armada wreck in Tobermory Bay on the Island of Mull.

opp. page: HMS Edinburgh. (Photo courtesy of the Imperial War Museum)

When Drake scattered the Spanish Armada in the autumn of 1588, the survivors headed north and attempted to round the north of Scotland and sail back to Spain from there. The story of their tragic wrecks on the Faroes and the West coast of Ireland is well known. One galleon, however, managed to find the safe anchorage at Tobermory and stayed there to recover and reprovision before returning to Spain. Although the name of this vessel is not exactly known, it was believed to be the *Florencia*. The captain traded with the McLeans of Duart for food and supplies and in return lent a number of his soldiers from the ship to assist the McLeans to prosecute some local disputes with his neighbours. Word eventually reached London that one of the Armada ships was anchored at Tobermory and Queen Elisabeth sent an agent to Mull to investigate. He managed to get on board the vessel and blow up the main magazine. The ship was torn apart in a great explosion with considerable loss of life. The cook, who was on deck at the time, was blown ashore and miraculously survived. The bay where he landed was known for many years as Cook's Bay and the actual spot now lies under the McBrayne's ferry terminal slipway.

The rights to the wreck were later granted in perpetuity to the Duke of Argyll and it was with his successor that we negotiated a contract to investigate the wreck. Mike Stewart took a team of divers and a barge with sophisticated dredging equipment to remove the mud overlaying the wreck. Sadly we found that what was left of the Florencia was completely broken up by many previous salvage attempts and were unable to obtain any positive identification of the ship.

In 1983 we were contacted by a German film company who had somehow managed to acquire permission from the Ministry of Defence to film the wreck of HMS *Hampshire* which lies off Marwick Head in the Orkneys. Her loss and the subsequent events are one of the abiding mysteries of the sea. In 1916, the Czarist regime in Russia was teetering and the British government decided to support them by sending an emissary with one million gold sovereigns to Russia. The emissary that they chose was none other than Lord Kitchener of Khartoum fame. He travelled north to Aberdeen by train with the sovereigns under armed guard, and took a ship to Scapa Flow in the Orkneys. The fleet was at anchor there, having just returned from the battle of Jutland. Kitchener was entertained at dinner on the flagship "The Grand Duke" by Admiral Jellicoe.

Kitchener had authority to commandeer any ship he wished for his trip. Apparently the *Hampshire* was the only ship that was both fuelled and armed. This was undoubtedly because she was already a very old battle cruiser, built in the 1890s, with an open bridge and had not taken part in the battle of Jutland. The weather that night was foul and the only available passage out of Scapa Flow was known to have been mined by German U-boats. Jellicoe tried to persuade Kitchener to wait until the morning and leave in daylight. Kitchener refused and insisted on leaving through the mined channel that evening.

The *Hampshire* sailed from Scapa Flow without incident and turned north up the west side of the islands. Towards the north end of the island off Marwick Head she struck a mine and started to go down. The Captain gave the order to abandon ship. In those days ships did not have a full complement of modern lifeboats and relied on primitive Carley Floats. The weather was bad and life expectancy in the water would only be an hour or two A survivor reported seeing Kitchener on deck in full uniform refusing all efforts to rescue him. Finally, all the crew either climbed onto Carley Floats or jumped into the sea as the *Hampshire* sank in 90 metres (300 feet) of water.

Back on Orkney the islanders were no strangers to tragedy at sea and flocked to the beaches to try to pull survivors from the surf. To their surprise and horror they were prevented by armed troops from reaching the beaches and helping the desperate crewmen. In the event very few men survived and Kitchener was not seen again, a sad and ignominious end for a man who had achieved so much in his lifetime.

At the end of World War I, there were a number of very acrimonious inquires in London about the loss of the *Hampshire*. There were serious allegations that the *Hampshire* was sunk on purpose to get rid of Kitchener, who was becoming an embarrassment to the government. It was also alleged that the shipment of gold sovereigns was more to help prop up the Russian industrial empires of some senior members of the Government. There is never smoke without fire, and there must have been some serious embarrassment in the corridors of Whitehall for the files were promptly locked up for 50 years. Malcolm and I, together with John Houlder, knew of the *Hampshire* story long before then and had been waiting in 1972 for the release of the *Hampshire* files. Unfortunately, the government decided not to release all the files in 1972. Why? What could be so sensitive after so many years? I can understand that, after the 1917 Russian Revolution, the British government had to come to terms with the new Soviet Union and would not want to publicise their so recent efforts to preserve the Czarist regime; but, 50 years later, who would really care?

The plot began to thicken in the late twenties when Navy divers started to work on the wreck, presumably to recover the gold. They had brought in a colourful American diver from New York named Courtney, who was also a locksmith. The wreck of the *Hampshire* was upside down. As the divers were cutting a way into it, they broke through a bulkhead into one of the coal bunkers. The coal bunkers were tanks on the outer sides of the ship in the same position as the fuel tanks on the *Edinburgh*. The divers were buried in an avalanche of coal and two of them perished. There is no documentary evidence of the gold being recovered, but we have to assume that it may have been.

It was a surprise to us that, of all nationalities, the MoD had given a permit to a German company to film the wreck. Their permission allowed them to film the remains of the *Hampshire* but to take nothing from the wreck itself. We entered into a contract with the German company and agreed to make available a diving support vessel with an ROV to film the wreck. In order to save cost, we agreed with the Germans to fit this in on our way back from a separate North Sea commercial diving job. We were just completing a diving job for Shell with a vessel called the *Stena Workhorse*, and planned to film the *Hampshire* on the way home. We finally arrived on the site on a Friday afternoon in good weather and positioned over the wreck with the vessel's DP system.

The ship is lying upside down in 90 metres (300 feet) of water. As the ROV descended, we could clearly see the name "*Hampshire*" written around her stern. At the bow, we found the remains of the damage caused by the German mine that sank her. We could see no trace of an explosion from the inside that would have caused steel plates to be bent outward, as opposed to being bent inward as would happen in the case of mine damage. The original damaged area had been considerably enlarged, presumably by the efforts of the navy divers in the twenties. We carried out detailed ROV survey of the exterior of the wreck and were then able to fly the camera through the interior of the ship. The internal bulkheads were wafer thin in places and we could simply drive the camera through them. Sadly, we could find no obvious trace of the gold sovereigns, worth more than £60,000,000 today. As we were not allowed to put divers into the wreck for a detailed search it is distinctly possible that they are still there. Somewhere in the locked-away archives there must be documentary evidence of where the gold was stored on the ship.

The government has consistently refused to allow anyone to dive on the wreck on the grounds that it is a war grave. This is a totally inadequate excuse used to keep people away, but for what reason? We know, from the papers that have been released, that all the crew got off the ship and were largely lost due to the weather, exposure, and lack of rescue facilities. When the *Hampshire* went to the bottom there were no men on board her at all (except perhaps Kitchener). I would love to know what the government has to hide after all these years. They are still extremely sensitive about it. Our presence on site was apparently reported at once by the Orkney Coastguards who in turn reported to the MoD in London. Fortunately we had arrived on a Friday afternoon and the coastguard could not get any response from the MoD because they are probably members of the "POETS" Society (Piss Off Early Tomorrow's Saturday).

It was midday the following Monday by the time the MoD started to call our office and ask us what we were doing. We found this somewhat strange, as the German film company had an agreement with MoD and we had told them by telex that we were going to the site. Again some very sensitive nerves were jangling. What is so secret about this wreck? Perhaps they know that the money is still there and don't want anyone to find it. If that is the case, why have they not used the Navy divers to recover it in recent years now that they have had much better technology and equipment available to them. The MoD seems to have an enormous inferiority complex about its own diving capability. Before the advent of saturation diving, the Navy led the field in air diving, and produced a generation of well-trained divers who have been the backbone of the commercial diving industry. Driven by the speed of developments in the North Sea in the early seventies, the commercial companies such as my own leapt ahead in technology, particularly in saturation diving, and dynamically-positioned diving support vessels. With the high North Sea wages, we were able to attract all the best and well trained divers away from the Navy.

In the early eighties, the Navy announced plans to build a diving support vessel of their own. This happened at a time when there was a glut of diving vessels on the market. We, together with several of our competitors, offered to sell the MoD existing and proven diving vessels complete with saturation diving systems for prices ranging from ten to twenty million pounds.

"No," said the MoD, "we have special requirements and will design and build our own vessel." We all then offered to supply them with saturation diving systems to put in their new ship.

"No," said the MoD, "we know better than you lot and will design and build our own."

Many years later the HMS *Challenger* was launched, but they could never get it or its diving system to work properly. They finally called in consultants from the diving industry, but it proved too much of an abortion to ever work properly. After an expenditure of taxpayer money of over £200,000,000, the Challenger was sold for less than £2,000,000, having never worked. This is yet another example of the British taxpayers' money wasted. Before the situation had become so disastrous I had the opportunity to meet the Chief of Defence Staff, Sir John Fieldhouse, when he gave a speech to the Anchorites club in London. When I talked to him about the *Challenger* and asked why they did not buy a commercially available vessel he became very agitated and called for his aides to "Get this diver away from me." When the navy wanted to salvage confidential material from the wrecks of HMS *Sheffield* and HMS *Coventry* after the Falklands war, they had to charter commercial diving ships.

By that Monday morning when the MoD was starting to get agitated, we had already completed the filming work. The wreck of the *Hampshire* is like a scrapyard of bronze and artifacts. There were a large number of these lying on the seabed near the wreck, together with a complete bronze propeller and shaft. The German's permission specifically precluded removing items from on the wreck, but not from the seabed around it. Therefore, they picked up the propeller and shaft and other artifacts from the seabed. These were reported by telex to the receiver of wreck in Aberdeen and duly handed over when the ship docked on her return.

The propeller and shaft lay on the quay side in Aberdeen for more than a year while the embarrassed authorities tried to decide what to with it. They asked us if we would put it back on the site for them (at our cost) to which they got the obvious reply. They finally decided to do what we had suggested when we raised it. The propeller and shaft were finally taken back to the Orkneys and erected on Marwick Head as a memorial to the brave men who lost their lives in that mysterious act of folly in 1916.

Keith Jessop, in the meantime, was taking a serious interest in more valuable Spanish shipwrecks. From the discovery of the New World in 1492, Spain managed to sustain a regular flow of gold and silver to maintain its economy until the late eighteenth century when the countries of South America progressively gained their independence, and Spain lost its stranglehold on the continent. For more than two centuries, the Spanish ran two Plate Fleets a year, the galleones which sailed from Cartagena, and the Flota which sailed from Vera Cruz in New Spain (Mexico). Their cargoes were predominantly silver, although a large quantity of gold and precious stones was also shipped. Spain became so dependent on this annual income that they never developed an industrial base of their own, choosing instead to trade their bullion with the low countries for consumer goods. The Dutch would then export the silver to the Far East to buy porcelain, tea and spices.

During the seventies, American treasure hunters had started to make some spectacular discoveries in Florida and the Bahamas. A great many treasure ships had been caught by hurricanes while making passage through the Florida Straits and were driven ashore to be broken up by the seas and overgrown with coral. Despite contemporary salvage efforts by the Spanish using native divers, there were still good finds to be made by modern divers. Each year in late summer the galleones and the Flota would meet up at the Cuban port of Mantanzas to victual and prepare for the dangerous journey back to the Guadalquivir river and Seville in Spain. Apart from the ever-present risk of autumn hurricanes, they had to face the navigational problems of sailing their lumbering fleet through the endless chain of islands and reefs stretching from the Bahamas in the north to Trinidad in the south. This was an easy task in good weather, but in storm conditions and at night it was lethal. The Spanish navigators could establish their latitude with some degree of accuracy, but their longitude could be tens or even hundreds of miles out due to their lack of accurate clocks. In addition to the natural hazards, the Spanish fleets were increasingly prey to an ever-growing army of pirates, corsairs, and privateers.

They had good reason to be concerned on this account. In August 1628, Dutch pirate Piet Heyn captured the entire annual Plate Fleet in Mantanzas Bay. He transferred the treasure to his own ships and, taking the four principal Spanish vessels as prizes, set sail for Holland. He lost three of the Spanish vessels on the south coast of Ireland in a storm, but managed to get all the treasure back to Amsterdam. He was knighted and made a Freeman of the city, but the wealth and honours could not save him when he was stabbed to death during a fight in a brothel two years later.

One of the Spanish ships lost near Castlehaven in Southern Ireland was the flagship, the *Santa Anna Marie*, with the Admiral Velasquez on board. He was rescued with most of the crew, but the ship sank in some 60 feet of water with more than 40 fine bronze cannons. In the summer of the following year, an English diver named Silas Jones arrived at the site with a rudimentary diving bell and managed to salvage all except 6 of the cannons. These were fought over by the Spanish, who claimed ownership of them, by the Dutch, who claimed to have taken them by a legitimate act of piracy, by the English, who claimed ownership of Ireland, and by the

locals, who were on the spot. People were killed fighting over the salvaged guns and what finally happened to them is not recorded. The Admiral Velasquez was finally ransomed back to Spain where, after languishing for several years in prison, he was finally tried for the loss of the fleet and publicly beheaded in Madrid. The remaining six cannons were raised in the seventies by local divers and are now believed to reside in private collections.

As if these perils were not daunting enough, the annual Plate Fleet finally had to run the gauntlet of the bar at Sanlucar de Barrameda that lay across the entrance to the Guadalquivir River. This passage claimed numerous treasure ships and their crews within a few miles of home and safety.

Keith Jessop used all his charm and persuasion to acquire an exclusive four-year contract to search for and salvage wrecks off the shores of the Turcs and Caicos Islands. This British Protectorate lies across the Plate Fleet route, stretching from the south of the Bahamas down to the north of the Abrajos Reef, now known as the Silver Banks, just to the north of Hispaniola. Keith had acquired research information which indicated that a number of Plate Fleet wrecks had been lost on the reefs to the west of the Turcs and Caicos Island chain.

We went into this project with Keith as an investor. Keith was still smarting about what he considered to be his very small percentage in the *Edinburgh* salvage. The Turcs and Caicos project required no deep-diving technology or equipment from the North Sea. Malcolm and I were at full stretch running our expanding business and could not devote any time to this latest project. We therefore agreed to a 50/50 share with Keith running the project. Keith also brought in a number of outside investors from the United States to provide additional funds.

Keith used the project's funds to buy and fit out a 30-metre (100-foot) motor vessel as the main base for the expedition. We soon realised that the crew seemed to consist of most of the Jessop family, which we were not very enthusiastic about. He then sailed the ship across the Atlantic to the Turcs and Caicos to begin the search. As usual Keith was characteristically optimistic about the expedition's prospects. He had acquired information on two specific wrecks reported lost on the Turcs and Caicos which had substantial recorded cargoes of silver. We also knew that the cargo manifests deposited in the archives of the Casa de Contratacion de las Indias (House of Trade of the Indies) in Seville detailed only the official cargo carried in each vessel. In fact, a vast quantity of unofficial treasure was carried on each vessel by the officers, crew, and returning passengers, all trying to bring back their own wealth from the New World without paying the "Quinta," the 20% tax to the Spanish Crown. We had in fact inadvertently stumbled on a rare and incredible first-hand account of this smuggling a few years earlier.

While we were in Guernsey researching the loss of the *Victory* we deduced that there must have been correspondence between people on the island and the Admiralty about the disappearance of the ship and the subsequent search for the wreck. One of the principal manors on the island was owned by the Saumarez family. This family has the unique distinction of providing more admirals for the Royal Navy than just about any other. We visited Cecil Saumarez in the early seventies to ask for his help in our search for the *Victory*. He very kindly gave us the run of his extensive library. While we were poring through his records, Cecil Saumarez appeared from a cupboard with an old shoebox packed with hand-written manuscripts. He had brought it out to show us, as he had seen the date of 1744, the year of the loss of the *Victory*.

We read through the documents with mounting excitement. Here was the original log of his ancestor Phillip Saumarez's circumnavigation of the world with Admiral Anson in 1744. The war of "Jenkin's Ear" had broken out in 1739, when Jenkin's ear was sliced off by a Spanish officer. As history would dictate, the government of Walpole took even more exception to this than the unfortunate Jenkins, and a serious war ensued.

Walpole sent a fleet under Admiral Vernon to attack Spanish possessions in the Caribbean and, almost as an afterthought, sent a fleet of seven ships under Admiral Anson to harry the Spanish trade in the Pacific and to capture the "Black Ship." This was the annual Galleon that carried the treasure from the Philippines to Acapulco. From there it was transferred to Carthagena in the Caribbean by mule train. The Anson voyage was ill-equipped, as the best ships and equipment went to Vernon for his Caribbean campaign.

Anson's fleet was comprised of four fourth raters: the *Centurion* of 60 guns, the *Gloucester* of 50 guns, the *Severn* of 48 guns, and the *Pearle* of 42 Guns. There also was a sixth rater (the *Wager*) of 24 guns, a sloop (the *Tryall*) of 14 guns, and two pinks (the *Anna* and the *Industry*) that carried supplies.

There was a desperate shortage of trained seamen to make up the ship's companies and no available marines. Half of all the seamen on board were rounded up by press gangs. This was still not enough and to make up the ship's complements they had to draft in 552 Chelsea Pensioners under the command of the doughty Colonel Cracherode, few of whom survived the trip. These old men were marched from Chelsea to Portsmouth, many in need of medical attention and some carried on stretchers. On arrival, the *Centurion*'s surgeon considered two of them too ill to go on board and sent them to the hospital. When the Admiralty heard of this, they accused them of shirking their duty and sent them straight back on board. They were both dead within a month. Of the seven ships and 1,939 men who started the voyage, 1,051 men died and only the flagship, the *Centurion*, completed the voyage.

Phillip Saumarez started the voyage as a 29-year-old third lieutenant on the *Centurion* and his younger brother, Thomas, was a lowly midshipman on the same ship. He joined the ship on December 25, 1739. On June 24, 1740, the fleet was finally ready to sail. As they were pulling out, they passed Admiral Balchen's *Victory* and fired a 17-gun salute. That was the same *Victory* that was to perish on the Casquets rocks off Alderney in 1744 with all hands.

Owing to sickness of the *Tryall*'s captain, Saumarez was put in command of her for the first part of the voyage until her captain recovered. The fleet of seven ships under Anson on the *Centurion* stopped to water at Madiera and then, after making landfall in

Brazil, followed the coast of South America down to Patagonia. It took the fleet a gruelling two months of storms and contrary winds to round the horn. During this appalling passage the fleet made no headway for days on end, crew members were lost overboard, and several suffered broken bones. The *Severn* and the *Pearle* gave up and turned back, eventually reaching Rio de Janiero to reprovision. In mid-April, while still struggling to round the horn, Saumarez was recalled as first officer on the *Centurion* as the *Tryall*'s captain had now recovered. On returning aboard, he was shocked to find that virtually everyone was infected with scurvy, 40 men had been lost already, and most of the crew were unfit to perform their duties. The old marines were all sick or dead. They were living in appalling conditions in their own filth, withstanding dreadful sea conditions. In late April they had a chance to clean below decks before being hit by another storm that took the *Wager*'s mizzen mast and parted the *Anna*'s forestay.

In May, having finally rounded the horn, the *Centurion* reached the previously agreed rendezvous point at the Island of Nuestra Senora de Socorro. Finding none of his ships there, he continued 150 miles north to the next planned rendezvous point at Chiloe Island. When he realised it was unlikely he would find any of them, he hurried 700 miles north to Juan Fernandez to try to save his ship and as many of his men as possible. On May 25, Saumarez wrote in his log, "most of our men being now so sick that we did not muster above 20 seamen in each watch. At the same time our sick dying a pace."

Due to a serious navigational error, it was not until June 8 that they finally arrived at Juan Fernandez. They estimated that the delay had cost them a further 100 lives from scurvy, but by being late they just missed a Spanish squadron that had been waiting to ambush them until a few days previously. When they arrived there were only six seamen fit to anchor the ship and all the officers and their servants had to assist.

Meanwhile, the *Wager* had also lost its foresail halyards and was struggling under jury rig. She was finally wrecked on an island that is now called Wager Island. Most of the crew survived the wreck and set up camp on shore. After the captain went mad and shot dead a midshipman, the crew mutinied and decided to make their own way back to civilisation. They cut a ship's boat in half on the beach and lengthened it to 50 feet. They renamed it *Speedwell*. Under a gunner called Bulkley, they managed to round the horn, leaving the captain and a few men on Wager Island. By a great feat of seamanship, Bulkley eventually arrived at Rio Grande with 30 survivors, most of whom made it back to England.

The party left on Wager Island were eventually rescued by friendly Indians, and by 1746 most of them finally arrived back in England.

At Juan Fernandez, Anson set up camp ashore and transferred the sick onto dry land to recuperate with fresh food. This was the island where Alexander Selkirk had been marooned from 1704 to 1709, and the remaining crew was able to find traces of his stay there. His story had inspired Daniel Defoe to write Robinson Crusoe. The island had plentiful food and was free from harmful insects. Once onshore, with access to fresh food, the men recovered quickly. Miraculously, on June 11, the *Tryall* arrived in a pitiful condition but still afloat.

On June 21, a sail was sighted trying to beat into the island. It then disappeared and it was not until June 27 that she was sighted again and a cutter was sent out to assist with fresh provisions. They found that the ship was the *Gloucester*, which had been turned into a floating charnel house with two-thirds of her men dead and hardly anyone able to work. Saumarez recorded "The dead on the *Gloucester* lay everywhere. Those who could walk or crawl did so with a most excruciating pain in their joints caused by the scurvy. Captain Mitchell and the men who still remained alive barely held onto life. Rats infested the ship, gnawing away at the dead and eating the fingers and toes of the sick who were too weak to defend themselves. A pestilence plagued the ship."

On August 27, the pink *Anna* arrived in good condition, having found a sheltered bay where they had recuperated with fresh food. This was in fact just north of Wager Island and is still called Bahia Anna Pink to this day. However, the ship itself was found to be rotten and beyond repair. She was stripped of serviceable parts and her crew were distributed among the other vessels. Anson stayed at Juan Fernandez until September, by which time he and his crew were fully recovered. He had cleaned all the ships and scrubbed the bottom of the *Centurion*, retightened her sheathing, and recaulked her. Of the marines only Colonel Cracherode and 17 men now remained alive. In his log, Saumarez commented "This man is indestructible." By now Anson feared the worst and assumed that the other ships were lost. On the September 9, he set sail to execute his orders "To harry the Spanish trade in the Pacific." On September 13, they captured a Spanish vessel *Nuestra Senora de Monte Carmelo*, which they took as a prize. The *Carmelo* was carrying a general cargo and some silver. Saumarez spoke fluent Spanish and, on questioning the *Carmelo*'s captain, he discovered that the Spanish had sent the famous Pizarro at the head of a fleet to chase him, but that they had failed to round Cape Horn. Even more distressing to

Saumarez was the fact that Vincent's expedition in the Caribbean had failed and the grand plan for them to join up at Panama an choke off the supply of gold from the New World to Spain had failed dismally.

They were now entirely on their own, dramatically weakened, and a very long way from home. Anson decided that they could not face another passage around the Horn but would sail across the Pacific to the Philippines to try to capture the annual Manila Galleon (the famous Black Ship), and from there sail home via India and the Cape of Good Hope. First Anson decided they would attack Acapulco. It was clear that the Spanish considered them all to be lost at sea and no longer to pose a threat. Saumarez was put in command of the *Carmelo*. Shortly afterwards the fleet captured three other Spanish merchant vessels and Anson scuttled the *Tryall* after her planks sprung and she was found to be beyond repair. Anson then decided, based on information from the captured crews, to attack the port of Payta in northern Chile. This raid yielded a considerable sum in treasure. They left the town in flames and continued up the coast toward Peru with their four prizes. They later met up with the *Gloucester* which had captured two more prizes and found more gold and silver in them.

Anson patrolled off Acapulco, waiting for the Black Ship until April 1742.

When it became clear that she was not there, they watered and provisioned at Chequetan in Mexico, in preparation for their long Pacific crossing. Anson reluctantly decided to scuttle the Spanish prizes and distribute the crews and stores between the *Centurion* and the *Gloucester*. In early May they set sail across the Pacific. The journey across the Pacific became another epic struggle against scurvy, with men dying like flies. They had somehow missed the trade winds and were frequently becalmed. In August the *Gloucester* began to leak badly. With the crew too weak to man the pumps, Anson transferred what he could to the *Centurion* and set the *Gloucester* on fire.

With the death toll rising daily, they continued to Guam, where once more they put the sick ashore to recuperate. The able-bodied men set about repairing the ship. One night, when Saumarez was on board with a skeleton crew, they were struck by a storm that broke her anchor cables and drove her helpless out to sea for five days. It was almost a month before Saumarez managed to sail her back to Guam to meet up with an eternally grateful Anson. Anson was so sure that the *Centurion* was lost that he had set about making a sailing boat to try to take the survivors the 1,500 miles to China.

They now rapidly reprovisioned the *Centurion* and set sail for Canton, finally arriving in the Macao roads in mid-November 1742. The appearance of a British Man of War in Macao caused chaos and consternation. Anson was to spend four frustrating months begging and cajoling the Chinese, the Portuguese, and the East India Company traders, for men and equipment to repair and revictual the *Centurion*. To allay the suspicions of the Chinese and Portuguese, he maintained that as soon as his ship was again seaworthy he would sail to Batavia and from there on to England.

When they finally left Macao in mid-April 1743, they had 237 officers and men. Anson had sent some of his spare officers back to England on an East Indiaman to carry his report to the Admiralty. He had also sent back the indomitable Colonel Cracherode as there were no marines left alive to command. Once at sea, Anson assembled the men and told them that they were going after the Black Ship. Despite being away from home for more than two years and suffering indescribable privations, the men were overjoyed. This was their one big chance for prize money. Anson sailed to Cape Espirito Santo in the Philippines to lie in wait for the Black Ship.

Having arrived there on May 19, they did not have long to wait. Despite the fact that the Spanish had found out that *Centurion* was there they did not change their sailing plan, being so confident of their advantage in size and numbers of crew. On June 20, *Centurion* sighted the *Nuestra Senora de Cobadonga*, the Black Ship. They gave chase and fought a brisk engagement for an hour at close range before the *Cobadonga's* captain struck his colours and surrendered. Anson sent Saumarez on board to accept the surrender and so, perhaps the greatest prize of all time fell to the Royal Navy.

He found the decks littered with corpses, entrails and severed limbs. Their onslaught had killed some 50 Spaniards for the loss of only three of the *Centurion's* crew. Saumarez was now given command of the *Cobadonga* to take it home as a prize. He only had a crew of some 50 men on the ship with hundreds of Spanish prisoners to keep under control. The *Cobadonga* was badly damaged from the engagement and taking water constantly. Saumarez patched up the vessel as best he could, but could not stem the leaks, which would require careening to fully inspect the hull. They set about transferring the treasure to the *Centurion*. They were constantly hampered by bad weather and were making for Canton and its sheltered anchorage to make repairs and take on provisions for the long journey home. Despite being so lightly manned, Saumarez had to keep the Spanish prisoners under 24-hour armed guard. The prisoners so heavily outnumbered the crew that they were insufficient men available to crew the vessel, carry out repairs, transfer the treasure to the *Centurion* and carry out a full search of the ship. Despite all these difficulties, by late June they had transferred so much weight of treasure to the *Centurion* that they had to put the upper deck guns into the hold as ballast to retain the stability of the ship.

The Spanish Crown charged a 20% tax on all bullion imports by private individuals from the New Word. This was know as the "Quinto" and evidence of payment was by a stamp on the bullion. The only thing that has not changed over the centuries is human nature. Accordingly, the human aversion to paying tax was just as active then as now. With life expectancy so much shorter in those days, coupled with the perils of the sea and of tropical diseases, the Spaniards usually only had one chance to enrich themselves. This they did with single-minded diligence and, in doing so, refined the art of smuggling to a high degree of perfection. I must admit to considerable sympathy with their cause after the problems that we faced with VAT some two centuries later.

Saumarez now set about searching chests in the hold and found these to have false bottoms hiding large quantities of smuggled gold and silver. As the weeks passed he was continually finding more treasure, much of it hidden behind false panels and false

ceilings in the ship. While going through the ship's stores, he became suspicious about the weight of the cheeses. On cutting these open he found them to contain solid gold bars. His log entry for that day stated, "This day found a large quantity of gold hidden in cheeses that we deemed exceeding heavy." By this time he had already transferred to the *Centurion* some 1,300,000 gold and silver dollars and thousands of pounds of gold and silver objects and bullion. Also, *Centurion* already had on board the treasure from the sack of Payta and the Spanish ships that Anson had taken off the South American coast and thousands of assorted valuables artifacts, jewellery, and tapestries.

Throughout August and September of 1743, the two ships were anchored off Canton and were resupplied and provisioned for the journey home. Throughout this period, Saumarez continued to find more treasure and transfer it to the *Centurion*. By December, Anson had reluctantly decided that the Cobadonga was not in a fit condition to sail back to England. Reluctantly they arranged to sell it to Portuguese merchants for a miserable 6,000 dollars. This was a bitter blow for Saumarez, not only did he lose his first command, but his own position as second in command of the *Centurion* had since been allocated to another officer.

The *Centurion* finally left Canton at the end of December, and after an uneventful journey finally anchored off the Isle of Wight in June 1744 some three years and nine months after their departure.

The survivors returned to an incredible welcome. It took 32 wagons to transport the treasure from Portsmouth to the Tower of London. Accounts of the total value vary but in today's values it would be more than £50,000,000, and at the time, was greater than the budget of the Royal Navy for that year.

As with so many such enterprises, the wrangling now started in earnest. Under the prize system the moneys were shared in the following manner:

One eighth to the Commander in Chief (Anson)
Two eighths to the Captain (Anson)
One eighth to the lieutenants, gunners, mates surgeons, pursers and chaplains.
One eighth to quartermasters, midshipmen and gunners mates.
Two eighths to the seamen, cooks, marines and coopers.

All concerned were wealthy beyond their wildest dreams and Anson was promoted to First Sea Lord. Saumarez was able to buy Saumarez manor in Guernsey where the family still lives today. However, by law, the supernumary officers were not entitled to a share. They very reasonably considered that they were due a share and took their case to court. After a long battle the High Court of the Admiralty found for the Supernumaries. There was an appeal to the Lords which they lost. This left a legacy of bitterness that soured such a great achievement.

Saumarez was further rewarded with his own command, the *Nottingham*, but in 1747 was killed by a French cannonball at the age of 34. He left a wonderful legacy in the shape of his log that gave one of the only contemporary eyewitness accounts detailing the extent of smuggling on the Spanish treasure ships. This is of great significance to present-day salvors in their search for sunken Spanish treasure.

The other great development that was a direct result of this voyage was a detailed medical study into scurvy which resulted in the discovery that it could be prevented by Vitamin C. This breakthrough undoubtedly saved thousands of sailors' lives.

THE HISTORY
OF THE *CONCEPTION*

CHAPTER 9

Our persistent attempts to get the government to pay us the outstanding monies due from the 1981 salvage were getting us nowhere, and the Soviets were still stonewalling about letting us return to the wreck. By now we were becoming very annoyed with the bureaucratic dishonesty that refused to pay us the contractual amounts due from the physical division of the gold in Murmansk. We were also beginning to hear unsettling rumours of Soviet diving activity in the Barents Sea that we felt must be an attempt by them to recover the remainder of the gold. The Salvage Association questioned the Soviets on our behalf and they denied the diving operations were connected with the *Edinburgh*. It was now 1984, and because the war in the Falklands was over, we were able to apply much heavier pressure on the Shipping Policy Division of the DOT for payment and for permission to return and complete the salvage.

opp. page: Survivors being loaded onto HMS Harrier.
(Photo courtesy of the Imperial War Museum)

It was not until December 1985 that the DOT finally said that they would give us permission to return to the wreck **provided** we agreed to drop all claims for monies due from 1981. How's that for political blackmail! The contract for the completion of the salvage work was finally signed in July 1986 and contained the following clause:

"The Contractor agrees not to bring any action against the Principals nor to pursue any claims for further payment by them or for damages resulting from the said contract of 5 May 1981."

By that date the outstanding principal and accumulated interest amounted to more that £200,000.

Ever since the completion of the first salvage I had been pressing to get an award for the divers. They had created a world record for Britain (in my opinion, the equivalent to a moon landing) and made a great windfall profit for the British Treasury. I wrote again to Mrs. Thatcher requesting that their efforts be recognised, only to be told that, "It was not considered to be appropriate."

As we prepared for the long, delayed return to the *Edinburgh*, things were not going so well with the Jessop family in the Turcs and Caicos. We were not getting reliable reports so Malcolm and I made a trip to the islands to see for ourselves what was going on. We were not surprised to find that the attractions of the night life ashore were proving too great for the crew of the salvage vessel. The Jessops and the rest of the crew were spending more time ashore in the bars talking about salvage than searching the reefs. They had found a few ballast mounds of early wrecks on the reefs but nothing of significance. Furthermore, we found that they had not accurately plotted the areas that they had already surveyed. We were becoming increasingly concerned that this area had been well worked at some time in the past, and that there would not be any valuable pickings on these easily accessible reefs.

In the research dossier that Keith had acquired was information about a Spanish Plate Fleet wreck that had been lost on a reef south of the Turcs and Caicos Islands, but still in their territorial waters. This reef lay just to the north of the Silver Banks, where an American team led by Burt Webber had found the remains of a major Plate Fleet wreck in 1978. We wanted Keith to investigate this isolated wreck, as we felt that it was much more likely to be unpillaged, and would focus the salvage effort on one target as opposed to the hit and miss beach-combing (and bar-combing) that they had done so far.

I started to research the wreck that Burt Webber had found and uncovered an amazing story that had many parallels with our own operation on the *Edinburgh.*

In July of 1641, the "Flota" or Plate Fleet of New Spain (Mexico) left Vera Cruz for Spain. The Almiranta, or flagship, of this fleet was a large merchant vessel *Nuestra Senora de la pura y limpia Conception.* The *Conception* had been built in Havana in 1620. In 1641, the fleet stopped in her home port of Havana to reprovision and prepare for the voyage back to Spain in the late summer of 1641. The fleet finally left Havana on September 20 and headed north through the Florida Straits. There they were struck by a great storm that overwhelmed three of the vessels and damaged and scattered the rest. The *Conception* was badly damaged and was taking on a great deal of water. The level in the hold was rising alarmingly and, to save the vessel, the captain ordered the mainmast cut away and guns jettisoned to lighten the ship. They were running helplessly south before the storm with only their foresail set. This soon blew away and their situation became hopeless.

At the height of the storm, a wave carried away the figurehead of Our Lady of the Conception and the crew knew they were doomed. No sooner had the priests on board given every one confession than the weather began to improve and they were able to rig a jury foresail and get the flooding under control. By this time their stores and gunpowder were under water and ruined. They would be at the mercy of any pirate or privateer. As the weather continued to get better, they decided to make for Puerto Rico where there was a Spanish garrison, and they could try to repair the ship.

After three weeks of painfully slow progress, a major dispute broke out between the captain and the pilots as to the ship's position. The captain felt that they were much too far west and wished to sail east for another week, but the pilots insisted that they were now due north of Puerto Rico and wanted to turn south at once. Under the law, the pilots prevailed. The captain called for a silver bowl of water to be brought on deck and washed his hands in public in front of the crew as the ship turned south to its doom.

On the night of October 31, the *Conception* grounded on the dreaded Abrojos reef to the north of Hispaniola. She grounded in fine weather, but the crew was unable to get her off before the weather got up and drove her further onto the reef, where she rapidly started to break up. They had only one ship's boat left after the storm, so the captain gave orders to build rafts for the crew and passengers to escape. During the night, the ship started to break up quickly and there were scenes of panic and several lives lost in the ensuing efforts to abandon ship. The captain and some 30 of the senior

officers left on the longboat, leaving the remaining 450 or so passengers and crew to their own devices. They set about completing a total of 10 rafts, some taking as many 70 survivors. Three of the rafts were lost completely and on two others there was great loss of life from sharks swimming onto the rafts to pull victims into the sea. Two of the rafts were intercepted by English pirates who stripped the passengers of their clothes, valuables, and shoes and sent them on their way. The survivors had to make their way barefoot and naked over the mountains of Hispaniola (the Dominican Republic) until they were eventually rescued. About 30 men stayed with the ship until it finally sank and then left on a makeshift raft. Of these only two made it ashore and one of those was taken by a shark while going back into the shallows to rescue a floating water barrel. Altogether some 300 lives were lost and about 190 saved.

Throughout the winter of 1641-42, Villavicencio, the admiral of the *Conception*, fought the local bureaucracy to try to arrange for a salvage attempt. After months of futile effort, he finally gave up. The King of Spain was not prepared to spend any more money on the search for the *Conception*. In 1650, a Spaniard named Cavallero applied for a no cure, no pay contract to salvage the treasure, offering 66% of the proceeds to the Spanish Crown. He made two attempts to find the wreck in

1650 and 1652 and failed both times. Nothing more happened until 1665, when another Spaniard named Palacios applied for a contract. He failed after two expeditions to find the wreck site. The wreck was all but forgotten until 1683, when a colourful Boston-born sea captain called William Phips arrived in London. Phips had learned of the wreck of the *Conception* and apparently acquired a map from a survivor of the shipwreck. With the same missionary zeal shown nearly 300 years later by Keith Jessop, he was convinced that he could both raise the money needed to find the *Conception* and salvage the wreck. Amazingly, he persuaded Charles II to provide him with a ship to search for the *Conception*. This first expedition failed and Phips returned after Charles II had died and faced an uphill struggle to persuade King James to support him for a second expedition.

With his great powers of persuasion, Phips managed to get the Duke of Albermarle, Sir John Narborough, together with a group of wealthy investors, to back him. For his part, King James granted an exclusive Royal Warrant to Albermarle to exploit the wreck of the *Conception* in exchange for 10% of the proceeds being paid to the Crown (one wonders on what authority he was able to dispose of a Spanish treasure).

With this level of backing and a Royal Mandate, Phips was able to sail in 1686 with two ships, the *James and Mary*

under his command, and the *Henry* under Francis Rogers, his second in command. When they arrived in the Caribbean, their first priority was to trade with the settlers. They had carried a lot of trade goods with them to help fund the costs of the expedition. While Phips traded in Hispaniola, he sent Rogers in the *Henry* to carry out a preliminary search for the wreck. Rogers sailed to the north side of the Ambrosian Bank (the Abrojos) and tried to look for landmarks that had been described to Phips by a survivor of the *Conception.*

After finding an area of the reef that seemed to fit the description, Rogers anchored the *Henry* and sent out a ship's boat with a diver to start the search. The diver spent all day searching and at the end of the day they moved the *Henry* along the reef to continue the search the following day. The next day was January 20, 1647, and, after only a few hours, the boat returned with the diver to announce that they had found the wreck. They seemed to have had luck similar to ours with the *Edinburgh,* when it came to finding the wreck. They had about the same area to search and found their wreck in about the same time. The wreck was already covered in coral with virtually all the timber eaten away. They had no high-tech aids to help them, only the human eye of the divers. They were only able to find the wreck site by the cannons.

After recovering some silver bars and several thousand silver coins, Rogers decided to sail back to Puerto Plata to pass on the good news to Phips. When Rogers arrived, he went on board the *James and Mary* and, with a long face, proceeded to tell Phips what a hopeless job it was going to be and how they had failed to find anything at all. Rogers had surreptitiously slipped a silver bar under the table and eventually Phips knocked it with his foot and asked "What is this?"

"Oh, just something we found on the reef," said Rogers.

"Thank God, we are saved," said Phips; exactly my sentiments that night when Marion Williams had called me with the long awaited "Dog 36" 294 years later.

Phips and his crew worked full time whenever the weather permitted to break up coral and recover silver. He had only four native divers and these soon began to tire. After about two months on the wreck, two small vessels arrived that were also looking for the wreck. Pragmatically, Phips could see the advantage of using their divers to speed up the recovery work. He used his Royal Warrant to claim sole rights to the wreck and reached an agreement with the newcomers to work for him.

Once the deal was completed, the rate of recovery really accelerated and on some days they managed to recover more that a ton of silver. To further speed up the work they used a crude diving bell that provided a refuge with a seat where the divers could rest and breathe and even drink brandy that they had taken down with them. This was basically just an upturned tub, weighted at the base, that trapped a pocket of air as it was lowered. The air would last for an hour or two of use as a diver refuge until it became foul. The "bell" was returned to the surface and flushed out with fresh air.

By the end of April 1687, Phips had recovered 25 tons of silver and 25 pounds of gold. His divers were exhausted and it was time to go. Before leaving he swore the others to secrecy and agreed to meet them back on the wreck site at the start of the following season. Phips arrived back in England on June 6 to a tumultuous welcome. His exploits were the talk of the country. At least in those days, the State welcomed a record-breaking achievement. The *James and Mary* was taken to Deptford where she was put under Customs guard to protect the King's 10%. Albermarle and the other backers met the ship amid great rejoicing. The crews of the *James and Mary* and the *Henry* all received a share and each man was presented with a silver medallion. We had not known this when Malcolm and I commissioned the gold ingot necklaces for our divers, but it is nice to know that in those more ruthless times Phips had the same consideration for his men.

Phips was called to Windsor to relate the story to the King, who then knighted him and, as Sir William Phips, appointed him as Provost Marshall of New England. It is a pity that the palace could not see fit to follow that precedent and honour the *Edinburgh* divers. The value of the treasure recovered at that time was about £240,000, which would be many millions in today's money. Surprisingly, Phips share was only £11,000. When the King, Phips, and the crews had obtained their share, the rest was physically divided into eighths, which was the unit of division of the expedition's backers. A one-eighth share cost £400 and returned for the investor £20,000.

Albermarle and his fellow investors held a great dinner of thanks at the Swan Tavern in London. At this party, the crews were given their silver medallions and Phips was given a gold medallion. The backers set about planning a new expedition. This time King James was determined to get a better share. He offered to provide a frigate for protection, but pushed his share up to 20%. By an amazing coincidence, the frigate was called the *Foresight*. It seems that even long-ago governments still wanted an exorbitant amount of money to provide frigates to guard treasure salvage ships. This expedition was much better equipped. Phips commanded a large merchant vessel called *Good Luck and a Boy*. They also had the *James and Mary* and the *Henry* which had been refitted for the voyage. The faithful Rogers was now in command of another ship called the *Princess*.

Albermarle, who was to accompany them, fell ill, and delayed the departure considerably. This delay was to cost them dearly. When they finally arrived at the site in December 1687, there were some 30 boats and more than 100 divers working on the wreck. This is an incredible number to have assembled in such a remote and dangerous area so long ago. With the help of the *Foresight*, they were able to clear the intruders away and get back to work. They had no idea how much treasure had been taken by them, but estimated at least another 25 tons.

By now they had cleared the forward part of the vessel down to the hull timbers. According to reports from survivors, most of the treasure was stored aft of the mast, so Phips now turned his attention to this area. The stern area was covered in coral and despite heroic efforts the divers were unable to get at the mother lode. Phips even tried to use explosives by lowering a barrel of gunpowder with a primitive fuse onto the wreck. Perhaps fortunately for Phips and his crew, the charge failed to go off. Otherwise, the *James and Mary* may well have gone the way Quaglia's *Artiglio* on the Egypt salvage. Sir John Narborough fell ill and died, and was subsequently buried at sea on the site of the wreck that had made him rich. The expedition returned home having barely covered its costs and leaving a considerable quantity of silver still buried in the coral of the Silver Banks.

Having read that account of the relentless efforts that went into salvage so long ago, I doubted very much whether Jessop would find anything in the Turcs and Caicos and, indeed, he never did. He managed to exhaust all the investor's funds and then gave up.

In 1697 Daniel Defoe wrote his "Essay on Projects" in which he spoke of Phips's expedition as follows:

"Witnes Sir William Phips's voyage to the wreck; 'twas a mere project, a lottery of a hundred thousand to one odds; a hazard, which if it had failed, everbody would have been ashamed to have owned themselves concerned in a voyage that would have been much ridiculed."

That quotation was still true in 1981 regarding our expedition to the *Edinburgh.*

Phips went on to be Governor of New England and died a wealthy, and, no doubt, content man.

Burt Webber's subsequent efforts on the wreck of the *Conception* were a great success. He negotiated a no cure,

no pay contract with the Dominican Republic for 50% of the recovered treasure. He found the stern of the *Conception* beneath the coral and recovered approximately £20,000,000 of treasure. This was the largest haul in the <u>Guinness Book of Records</u> until it was eclipsed by the *Edinburgh* salvage.

With most of the wrecks in shallow water having been exploited, the diving industry now turned its attention to those Plate Fleet wrecks that were lost in deep water where they were definitely out of the reach of contemporary salvage efforts. These wrecks are much more difficult to find, as they have little or no iron in them to register on a magnetometer (a metal detector measuring magnetic anomalies). There are no living survivors to give details of where the ships sank, and large areas have to be searched. Furthermore, the wrecks, being wooden, have largely collapsed. While they are too deep for coral incrustation, if they landed on a soft seabed the precious metals could have sunk deep into it, making location and recovery very difficult.

There has been a dramatic increase in the technical capabilities of ROVs and their application to deep salvage. At the time of writing this book, a Florida-based company has just located a Spanish wreck in 1,500 feet of water in the Dry Tortugas and has recovered gold, pearls and porcelain from it using an ROV. This capability will bring into reach one of greatest unfound treasure ships of all time, the *San Jose*.

The *San Jose* was the Almiranta of the Flota that left Porto Bello on the north coast of South America (modern day Columbia) in 1708. At the time, the Spanish were suffering serious deprivations from the British, the French, the Dutch, and assorted pirates, privateers, and freebooters. The situation was further confused by Britain being at war with France. So great was the risk to their convoys that they had not sent one for two years. By 1708, Spain was desperate for the money and large amounts of precious metals and jewels had been gathered at Porto Bello awaiting shipment to Spain.

A strong fleet of 13 ships finally sailed in June, led by the *San Jose* of 64 guns under Admiral Count de Cass Alegre. Cruising offshore, waiting to intercept them, was a British squadron under Commodore Wager, comprised of his flagship the *Expedition*, the *Portland* under Captain Windsor, the *Kingston* under Captain Bridge, and a fire ship. Wager gave the signal to attack and, despite being heavily outnumbered he manoeuvred alongside the *San Jose* to engage her with his full broadside. After a heated exchange in which he rapidly gained the upper hand, disaster struck. An unlucky shot must have hit the *San Jose*'s hanging magazine in the bows, for she blew up as violently as the *Florencia* had in Tobermory back in 1588. The *San Jose* sank immediately, and Wager only managed to pick up two Spanish survivors. As it was, he barely managed to save his own ship. His decks were swept by burning debris which caused injuries to his men. More seriously, the tidal wave from the explosion poured water into his open gun ports. With guns run out the ship became unstable and nearly capsized. By the time Wager brought the ship back under control, the remainder of the Flota was hull down on the horizon. Undeterred he gave chase and managed to catch up with the *Santa Cruz*, of 50 guns, under the command of Count de Bega Florida. Despite the damage to his own ship, Wager managed to capture the *Santa Cruz*. He was fully occupied with his prize and 300 Spanish prisoners and had to leave the rest of the fleet to the *Kingston* and the *Portland*.

To Wager's fury, he found that they had not only failed to follow him into the attack, but had also failed to follow up the advantage resulting from the destruction of the *San Jose*. His other two ships had not aggressively chased the remaining Spanish ships and had allowed them to escape into Cartagena. In doing so, they had allowed one of the richest fleets to slip through their fingers. On his return to Port Royal,

Commodore Wager instituted Court Martial proceedings against captains Windsor and Bridge for dereliction of duty and they were both relieved of their commands.

Wager was promoted to Admiral and knighted, and he became wealthy from his share of the treasure from the *Santa Cruz*. He well knew that the greatest cargo was on the *San Jose* and she was now beyond reach and soon forgotten.

The officially-recorded cargo of the *San Jose* was enormous by Plate Fleet standards and, as Saumarez showed on the *Conception*, the official cargo would be almost doubled by the smuggled treasure. The only reason that this exceptional wreck has not yet been found and salvaged is because no one has been able to negotiate an acceptable contract with the Colombian government. Sooner or later, with patience and new technology, that great treasure will see the light of day once again.

RETURNING
TO THE *EDINBURGH*

CHAPTER 10

Once we had submitted to the British Government's blackmail and agreed to drop our claim for the outstanding monies from the first contract, the pace of affairs speeded up. Keith had always stoically maintained there was a total of ten tons of gold on the *Edinburgh*. Malcolm and I never believed this. If more bullion had been put on the vessel, then someone would have signed for it. Keith was basing his information on a statement by the Soviet Admiral Golovko in his memoirs. He stated that "The *Edinburgh* sank with ten tons of our Soviet gold." Keith was like a starving dog with a bone about this supposed additional four and a half tons and eventually began to believe his own publicity. He succeeded in so winding up the two governments about it that they added a new clause to the contract to the effect that they would get 60% if any more gold was found than the original five

opp. page: The modern diving support vessel Deepwater 1.

and a half tons. There was no justification at all for this, just more governmental greed.

The Soviets now insisted on another freebie trip to the West. They considered it essential to come back to Aberdeen to vet us technically before we went back to the wreck. What an insult!

We set about planning the return in meticulous detail. We faced a vastly different situation than the one we faced in 1981. We now knew the wreck and what equipment we needed, so we no longer had the fear of the unknown. However, the upside was vastly different; only 34 bars worth about £3,500,000 instead of 465 bars worth £50,000,000 remained on the wreck. We could no longer afford to give investors a five-to-one return, but we no longer needed risk sharers, we could afford to do the job on our own.

Since 1981, Malcolm and I had built two very large state-of-the-art dynamically-positioned diving support vessels, the *Deepwater 1* and *Deepwater 2*. These were twice the size of the *Stephaniturm* and fitted with enormous diving systems that would allow us to operate two divers outside the bell all the time. We now had built-in gas recovery systems, and much more powerful and sophisticated diver heating systems. All the elements of mystery were gone. For the divers, it would be relatively routine work, as other trail-blazers had paved the way and proved that it could be done.

The other big change in five years was that we now had satellite communications and could do away with the laughable dogs, kennels, and keepers. Igor Illyn was to join us again and David Keogh, but there would be no press at all, and Keith Jessop was not going either.

If we made one mistake with our divers in 1981, it was that we had selected the superstars of the industry, but we had not paid any attention to their physical fitness. That oversight cost us valuable time in the first operation as their physical fitness began to fail toward the end of the operation. This time we would select well-proven divers who were generally younger and fitter men. However, for continuity, we definitely wanted to have some of the original team along to pass on their valuable experience to the new team.

The new superintendent was to be Larry Kelly, who was one of our North Sea superstars and had been working the Deepwater boats since their launch. He naturally wanted to put together a crew that he knew and had worked with. Therefore, he was reluctant to include divers from the previous trip in his own team. After a great deal of negotiation, only Dougie Mathison was included in the crew list.

This operation was funded entirely from our own resources. The divers were on normal pay rates with a very generous performance bonus. We used our own ship and provided all the supplies and consumables ourselves. The crew for this operation was as follows:

Superintendent L. Kelly
Assistant Superintendent D. Cambell
Diver C. Rimmer
Diver D. Syme
Diver D. Degener
Diver D. Lane
Diver D. Moore
Diver G. Harper
Diver C. Blaylock
Diver J. Chisholm
Diver D. Mathison
Diver M. Weldon
Diver J. Grierson
Diver P. Dobbs

We mobilised the *Deepwater 2* in Peterhead in the middle of August 1986. Just one hour before the ship sailed the police arrived, went straight to Dougie Mathison's cabin, "found" some drugs, and hauled him off the ship. The timing was brilliant, by the time news reached us in Aberdeen it was too late to find a replacement and the ship sailed with no members of the original crew aboard.

The alarm bells were now ringing loud-ly in our office. Dougie Mathison was a most upstanding and well-educated

West Coast Scot who did not even smoke, let alone take drugs. Fortunately, it did not take long for the police to figure out that this was a set-up to get him off the ship, but we would never be able to find out who was responsible.

When the ship arrived on location and the diving started, they found the wreck as they had left it, except that an underwater camera, that had been left attached to the wreck in 1981 was missing. It seemed that the Soviets were suspicious that we had left sophisticated listening devices on the wreck and gone back themselves to investigate. Only they could have removed the camera. There was no evidence of any disturbance on the wreck in the bomb room area. It lay just as the pioneering team had left it, five years before. The Soviets must have removed the camera using an ROV with a manipulator.

The first instruction for the divers was to recover the five bars in it that the previous team had set aside ready to lift on the next dive, when Mike Stewart had called a halt to operations in October 1981. Here the confusion and obfuscation began. There was no news of the five bars despite our repeated requests. Finally, bars started to come up in ones and twos and Kelly said that there was no distinct group of five bars waiting to be lifted. If there was, then the Soviets must have taken them

along with the camera. Malcolm and I debated this at length and spoke to the previous divers. Someone was being economical with truth, but who? We could not see what the divers from the first trip had to gain by giving us false information. The only way to be really sure was to completely clear the bomb room and see how many bars we ended up with.

This proved to be a long and arduous job. The divers had to clean out every corner and every nook and cranny to make sure that we had left no bars behind. The last few proved very elusive. Some must have really been flung around in the sinking and were stuck with congealed fuel oil into the webs of steel beams. When we had finally scraped the cupboard bare, Larry Kelly reported that we had 29 bars — exactly five short of the 34 that should have been there and five short of the 465 that Captain Faulkner had signed for. Where were they? Malcolm and I were by now 100% sure that there had been 465 bars in the bomb room when the *Edinburgh* sank and that none were thrown out of the bomb room during the sinking. Had the 1981 team taken them, had the Soviets taken them or had this team misappropriated the five bars that were "ready to lift?" We decided to say nothing until we knew much more about the problem. It was particularly important not to let the press get a hint of our suspicions, as they would blow it out of all proportions and jump to all the wrong conclusions. Thank God Penrose was not on board.

As soon as the bomb room was clear, we decided to stay on site for a day or two and look for the mythical four and a half tons of gold Keith was convinced still lay in the *Edinburgh*. With the aid of a lump hammer, the divers managed to undo the dog latches on the watertight door that led to the companionway and lift shaft. The same shaft down which the gold had been lowered in Murmansk all those years ago. This was the door that had held back the sea and helped keep the ship afloat after the first torpedo strike. The divers used a hand-operated winch to pull the door open and it still swung back on its hinges.

The corridor outside the bomb room was completely clear, and directly opposite was the watertight door leading into the fuse store. Using the lump hammer again, the divers freed the dog latches and, as the door opened downward, they were able to push it open. The fuse room was completely undamaged and there, lying in a heap at the bottom were piles of wooden boxes. Amid mounting excitement the divers hauled these boxes one by one up onto the side of the hull. These boxes were about 50 feet down from the hole in the hull of the cruiser and lifting them out was a back-breaking job. Excitement turned to disappointment as each was found to contain fuses.

So much for Keith's dream of 10 tons of gold. I have learned with salvage that you have to have impeccable research with documentary evidence of what you are looking for. You must not believe rumours and suppositions, and never spend money without substantial evidence. You must work only from known and provable facts.

On the *Deepwater 2*, we had a very small ROV that was able to carry out a detailed survey of the wreck while the salvage work was underway. We particularly wanted to find the ship's bell. Divers always consider this to be the heart of a wreck, and certainly the most sought-after artifact. The bell invariably has the ship's name on it and is then ultimate proof of identity. Much as I would have loved the bell to grace my living room, this was one artifact that we would have to hand over to the Navy. Fortunately, the ROV was able to find it still hanging on the quarterdeck with its clapper intact. A diver had to hacksaw through its support bracket to remove it from the ship. The ROV also found the admiral's barge lying intact in the seabed. On each side of its bow were beautiful bronze crests of Edinburgh Castle. Larry Kelly knew Malcolm and I would love those as souvenirs and sent a diver down to recover them. Unfortunately, David Keogh saw this on the monitors and insisted on these being handed over to the Navy as well. Larry was a bit peeved to say the least, as we were paying the tens of

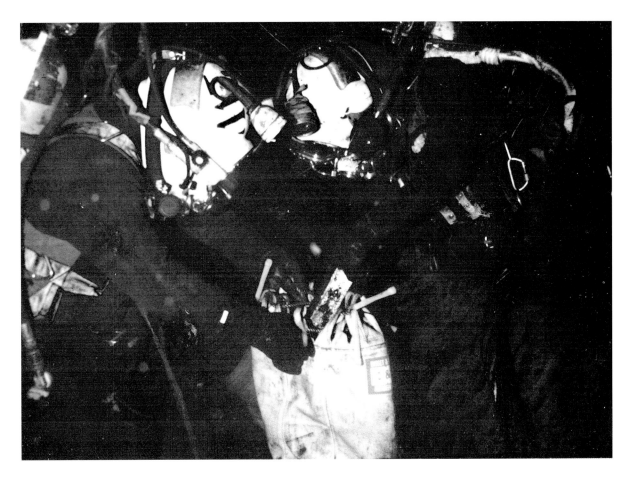

Divers loading gold bars into lifting sack.
(Photo by M. Stewart)

thousands of pounds a day that it cost us to be there and were entitled to some artifacts.

Most of the divers were ex-Navy and knew that the *Edinburgh* would have had two Admiral's barges, one on each side of the ship. This was because, when the ship was tied up to a jetty only one barge would be useable. Later that night

Larry ran a video of a previous dive on the monitors instead of the normal real time coverage. While that was going on he sent two divers to the other side of the wreck where they found the other barge and removed the plaques.

With the bomb room bare and the artifacts safely on board, it was time to assemble the ship's company on deck

Gunmetal door mat from the Bridge entrance to HMS
Edinburgh. *(Photo by R. Wharton)*

for a memorial service to honour the *Edinburgh's* dead. The service was again conducted by David Keogh for the Ministry of Defence.

Unlike the first trip, we were now much wiser in the devious ways of governments and tax collectors. The VAT postponed accounting treatment had been scrapped following the Brinksmat affair so we refused absolutely to be paid in gold and insisted that both Governments paid us in cash. We also refused to take the *Deepwater 2* into Murmansk, as we were on a tight budget this time and did not want to incur an extra two days of vessels costs on a pointless voyage. We therefore carried out a physical split of gold bars between the Soviets and the British government on board the *Deepwater 2.*

*Ric Wharton with the ship's bell found by
the 1986 expedition. (Photo by R. Wharton)*

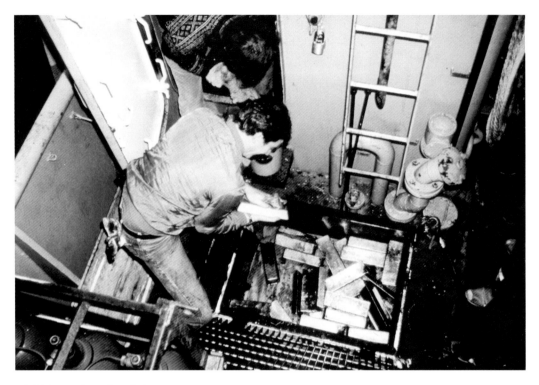

*Gold being cleaned up before
storage. (Photo by M. Stewart)*

*Wooden box that contained five gold ingots —
one of 93 from the wreck.
(Photo by R. Wharton)*

The MoD representative, David Keogh, logging in gold ingots. (Photo by M. Stewart)

Malcolm Williams, Rich Wharton, and Jerry Lynnes
with ingots from the 1986 expedition.
(Photo by R. Wharton.)

John Clarke "dreaming."
(Photo by J. Clarke)

Emergency lantern from HMS
Edinburgh. *(Photo by*
R. Wharton.)

Above, Malcolm Williams and Ric Wharton presenting the bell to the captain of the present Edinburgh. *(Photo by R. Wharton.)*

Below, gold. (Photo by R. Wharton)

The modern diving support vessel Deepwater 1.
(Photo by R. Wharton)

More gold. (Photo by J. Clarke)

Divers recovering the HMS Edinburgh *bell.*
(Photo by M. Stewart)

Late that night, a Soviet Missile cruiser came alongside the ship, a crate containing their share of the gold was craned onto their deck, and they disappeared into the night as quietly as they had arrived.

The *Deepwater 2* now returned to Peterhead where a security truck with a police escort again took the gold to London. Malcolm and I were now faced

with a difficult dilemma. In an ideal world, we would have quarantined the ship on arrival and searched it from stem to stern. To do this effectively would have taken days and needed police help. That would have created massive adverse publicity for what might have been a false alarm. There are so many places on a ship as large and complicated as the *Deepwater 2* where 5 bars of gold could be hidden by resourceful divers. I once heard of a diver who was a gun collector and had acquired a Kalashnikov rifle in Africa. To get it home, he cut the top off an oxygen cylinder, put the rifle in it, welded the top back on and repainted the bottle. The bottle came back in a rack with ten others and he was then able to recover his souvenir at his leisure. On balance, we decided that it was better not to risk souring the operation by instituting a major search that was unlikely to be successful, especially since the missing bars may have been taken by the Russians. So we massaged the records and announced that we had recovered all the gold.

The second operation was both a financial and operational success. We had kept our costs very tight and had no investors to pay.

Jerry Lynnes and Malcolm Williams with bronze plaques from bow of the Admiral's Barge on HMS Edinburgh. (Photo by R. Wharton)

We had now completed a 100% salvage, which is unique in salvage operations. We had completed the largest and deepest salvage operation of all time, without any diving accidents. Our place in the Guinness Book of Records would be assured for a long time to come. Malcolm and I were able to cover up the missing bars publicly by confusion over the number originally loaded. As the months went by, rumours began to circulate about what had happened to the missing five bars. We certainly felt that Dougie Mathison had been deliberately set up to make sure that none of the original *Stephaniturm* crew were on board the *Deepwater 2*, but we are still not sure why.

Looking back on it now years after the event, my feelings have mellowed somewhat. We did very well out of the *Edinburgh* project thanks to the heroic efforts of the divers. If any of them did manage to get clean away with five bars, good luck to them.

But if I had known who they were in that autumn of 1986, I would have made the bastards walk the plank!

The Russian share of the Edinburgh *gold is transferred to a Soviet missile cruiser in the dead of night.*

EPILOGUE

EPILOGUE

The story you have just read stems from an incredible incident of bravery and suffering in the appalling conditions of the Arctic convoys during the last world war. It was not well reported at the time, and had it not been for the *Edinburgh's* cargo the story would have been lost in the fog of war, one more tragic incident among so many. The heroism and suffering of the *Edinburgh's* crew was on a par with that of the crews of the *Centurion* and the *Conception*. One wonders if the present generation could, and indeed would, endure such privations. I would like to think that we do still have a crew of patriotic young men such as those who excelled in the Falklands and in the Gulf War. They are a minority of today's youth, but it is comforting to know that the spirit is still there. It was that same spirit that drove the divers and crew in the *Stephaniturm* to achieve such a spectacular success.

opp page: HMS Belfast *at anchor. (Photo courtesy of the Imperial War Museum)*

I find it disheartening to compare the British government's reaction to our successful return with that of Sir William Phips and of Admiral Anson the crew of the *Centurion*. The aftermath of both those expeditions suffered from outbreaks of "Gold Fever" which is a fault of human nature that has not changed since gold was first discovered.

The big difference was that Phips and Anson returned to find a grateful government that rewarded them and their men and a press that lauded their efforts. How despicable it is that the behaviour of the British government, the Inland Revenue, the Customs and Excise, and of the Civil Service were so petty and dishonest. How pathetic it is that "journalists" such as Barry Penrose exist, who are more interested in trying to create scandal where none exists, rather that report such a great achievement with accuracy. How sad it is that Britain, which used to be "Great Britain," does not laud its national achievements. I leave it to the reader's imagination to consider how the whole project and its outcome would have been presented in Paris, had it been carried out by a French salvor with French divers!

The current bearer of the illustrious name HMS *Edinburgh* is a modern destroyer. One of my pleasant duties after the second phase of the salvage was to present to her captain the bell that we had recovered from our HMS *Edinburgh*. The bell is now in the

United Services Museum in Edinburgh. I was able to have a professional museum replica made as a lasting souvenir of our great adventure.

By 1987, someone in the MoD suddenly woke up to the fact that the advances in diving technology had put a great many Naval wrecks within the reach of the modern diver. The first we knew of this ministerial brain-wave was the proposal to enact new legislation in the guise of the "Protection of Military Remains Act." It was only by chance that this oddly named piece of legislation came to our attention. Beneath the fine-sounding title, the Act proposed to ban any British national from diving on any naval wreck anywhere in the world. There was no publicity about this and no prior consultation process with the diving industry or other interested parties at all. The title of the bill did not mention diving at all and it was clearly the intention of the government to slip this through the House of Commons before any interested parties in the diving industry heard anything about it.

By the time that we became aware of it was very late in the day and has shortly to come before the House. I immediately contacted the Earl of Onslow, a man of great intellect who is not adverse to taking a stand on issues of principle. The bill's sponsor was Lord Trefgarne, the then Minister of State for Defence Procurement. Malcolm and

I requested a meeting with him to express our concern on behalf of the British diving industry. If the Act became law, it would have prevented a British company, or anyone employing British divers from diving on any British naval wrecks anywhere in the world. However, it did not prevent any other nationality from doing so. I was finally able to speak briefly with Lord Trefgarne on the phone. He was very aggressive and made it clear that he would brook no interference with his bill. When I asked him why it did not prevent other nationalities from diving on British wrecks, he said that it was because they could not enforce the legislation against other nationalities. I requested a meeting which he very reluctantly agreed to and implied that if we interfered with the bill, my company would be blacklisted for future salvage work.

I passed this information on to Lord Onslow who offered to come along to the meeting to see fair play. When we duly arrived at the Ministry for the meeting, Trefgarne came out of his office and was shocked to see Onslow with us.

"This is a private meeting, you can't come in!" said Trefgarne.

"Well I am attending to see fair play," said Onslow. Trefgarne then tried to stop Onslow from entering his office, but Onslow said "I am bloody well going

Project superintendent Larry Kelly hands over the ship's bell to Lt. Cdr. Ken Napier of the present-day HMS Edinburgh, *watched by Malcolm Williams, Ric Wharton, and members of the* Edinburgh *crew.*

to attend to make sure that you don't try to put the arm on these people."

Trefgarne was forced to give in, which he did with very bad grace, and to hear us out. He was now forced to discuss the proposed legislation, and we were able to bring in the Association of Diving Contractors to represent the interests of the industry. After a great deal of bitter infighting, the government was forced to back down and to so water down the bill that it became ineffective. We still don't know what their deeper motive was, or who in the government is so concerned about it. The whole subject is hypocritical. When merchant vessels are lost on military duty, they are not protected as war graves, even though their crews were fighting the same war and dying in the same way.

My abiding anger remains with the failure of the corrupt and prejudiced British Honours System for failing to recognise the achievement of our divers. This was particularly highlighted in the early nineties when the chairman of our former American partner's British subsidiary company was awarded a Knighthood for "Services to Industry." Some uncharitable observers have suggested that the award may have had more to do with his ability to lend his company's aircraft to the Conservative Party to ferry ministers around during the last election campaign.

I am sure ministers would never be influenced by such considerations. Perish the thought!

APPENDIX 1

On the surface, we are all subjected to the weight of some 15,240 metres (50,000 feet) of atmosphere (air) above us. This applies a pressure of 14.7 pounds per square inch (psi) or "one atmosphere." Air is approximately 80% nitrogen and 20% oxygen. The nitrogen is inert and purely serves to dilute the vital oxygen and deliver it to the lungs.

Because of these percentages, on the surface, nitrogen exerts 0.8 of an atmosphere of pressure inside the lungs, and oxygen exerts 0.2 of an atmosphere. It is important to remember these figures as they fundamentally control deep-diving technology and development.

Water is much more dense than air. A column of water 10 metres (33 feet) high weighs as much as all the atmosphere above our heads, so when a diver descends to 10 metres his body is subjected to a pressure of 2 atmospheres.

During World War II, the naval divers and human torpedo drivers had breathing sets using pure oxygen that was purified and re-breathed to avoid leaving a trail of telltale bubbles. There were numerous reports of accidents when the divers went deeper than 9 metres (30 feet).

When the human body breathes oxygen at 2 or more atmospheres, it becomes poisonous. Some people are more susceptible, and can succumb to oxygen poisoning at lower pressures.

A diver breathing pure oxygen subjects his lungs to 2 atmospheres pressure of oxygen at 10 metres. When he is breathing air, the pressure of oxygen in his lungs reaches 2 atmospheres at a depth of 90 metres (297 feet). This is the theoretical limit of air diving. Air, however, has other serious problems for the diver. Nitrogen, when breathed at high pressure is very narcotic, with immediate symptoms of drunkenness. Fortunately, the symptoms subside as soon as you come up, and there is no "hangover."

The other problem is that nitrogen is very dense, and when compressed, it becomes so thick that the body has to do a lot of work just to suck it into the lungs and expel it. This tires the diver quickly and is very dangerous.

I was certainly suffering from both these problems when we made the dive at Zlendi. It is for good reason that the legal limit for commercial air diving operations is now 50 metres (165 feet).

APPENDIX 2

Helium is a much lighter gas than nitrogen, so its density does not prove to be such a problem at great depths. Also, and most importantly, it is not narcotic. The problem of oxygen poisoning was solved very simply by reducing the percentage of oxygen in the mixture. For example a mixture of 10% oxygen and 90% helium would enable a diver to descend to 20 atmospheres, or 190 metres (627 feet) before the oxygen content became poisonous. The problem that then arises occurs on the surface; that mixture does not have enough oxygen to support life. This has to be overcome by starting the mixture at 20% at the surface and changing the mixture as the diver descends. This concept can be pushed deeper and deeper by reducing the oxygen content until at about 455 metres (1500 feet) the helium becomes too dense to breathe for a working dive.

All this we were learning, and learning the hard way, in the field.

When a diver breathes air under pressure, the inert nitrogen is absorbed into the body tissues. The amount absorbed is dependent on the depth and the time that the diver spends at that depth. This is like the dissolved gas in a bottle of fizzy water. If you take the cap off quickly, the water froths as the gas comes out of its solution in bubbles.

If you take the top of the water bottle very, very slowly, you can get the water to go flat without any bubbles forming. This is what you try to do when you decompress a diver. You bring him up slowly so that no bubbles of nitrogen form in the bloodstream. Bubbles are what cause the bends, so called because when travelling through the blood vessels they cause divers joints to 'bend' with the pain.

When we replaced nitrogen with helium, we found that helium under pressure was much more readily absorbed by the body tissues than nitrogen and consequently, it was harder to remove safely. This made the decompression much longer and more difficult to control.

Up until that time, divers had taken their decompression stops by simply stopping at the appropriate depth for the right length of time. Even when tenders supplying the diver with air or heliox (helium/oxygen mixture) by hose from the surface, the decompression times for deep diving became too long for comfort and safety.

On commercial oilfield contracts, this held up the work and was beginning to make diving uneconomic. The divers tended to work from pipe lay barges or crane barges that cost thousands of dollars an hour to operate and could not afford to stand idle while divers decompressed in the water.

The diving industry soon began to appreciate the positive advantages of helium: its lack of narcotic effects at depth, and its low density that allows it to be inhaled and exhaled down to about 455 metres (1,500 feet) without much difficulty.

We soon realised that, while the rate of absorption of helium into the body tissues was dependent on the depth and the time of exposure, the body tissues soon reached a saturation point after which no additional helium could be absorbed.

This meant that whether you put a diver down for a few hours or a month, the decompression time would be the same. All that was required then was a way to store the divers at pressure on the surface and transport them safely to and from the seabed.

APPENDIX 3

The pages within this appendix are copies of the original insurance policy and the liability insert, along with its various clauses.

APPENDIX 1

TYPE:	CARGO.
FORM:	S.G. Slip policy.
ASSURED:	Jessop Marine Recoveries Ltd., and/or British and/or USSR Government Authorities for their respective rights and interests.
PER:	Salvage craft "STEPHANITURM" and/or conveyances.
VOYAGE/INTEREST:	Salvage of gold bars in sunken vessel HMS "EDINBURGH" in Barents Sea and delivered part to Murmansk and part to Aberdeen (via Murmansk).
LIMIT:	£75,000,000 in all.
BASIS OF VALUATION:	Premium payable on the daily amounts receipted calculated at the mean of the London a.m. and p.m. Gold fixings that day. Amount of claim payable calculated on the mean of the London a.m. and p.m. Gold fixings on day of loss.

CONDITIONS:

Subject to:-
Institute Cargo Clauses (All Risks) CL80 1.1.63.
as far as applicable including War.
Strikes, Riots and Civil Commotions as per Institute Clauses.
Notwithstanding anything contained in the Institute Clauses referred to herein to the contrary this insurance attaches from the time the interest insured is landed on board the salvage craft and such interest have been receipted by officials on board vessel and continues until such time as the interest insured is delivered as follows:-
1) USSR interest free alongside Murmansk.
2) British Government interest free alongside Aberdeen.
3) Salvors interest. Aberdeen and 10 days after arrival security to be approved by underwriters prior to discharge.

Subject approval of security for stowage on vessel.

PREMIUM:

Payable on total value of actual amount of gold bars salved
rate 1) .10%   )
     2) .1125%   3) .125%) inclusive of war at scale.

Daily accumulation of gold bars salved to be advised to underwriters.

No Cure, No Pay — Insurance Policy

IMPORTANT

LIABILITY OF CARRIERS, BAILEES OR OTHER THIRD PARTIES

It is the duty of the Assured and their Agents, in all cases, to take such measures as may be reasonable for the purpose of averting or minimising a loss and to ensure that all rights against Carriers, Bailees or other third parties are properly preserved and exercised. In particular, the Assured or their Agents are required:—

1. To claim immediately on the Carriers, Port Authorities or other Bailees for any missing packages.
2. In no circumstances, except under written protest, to give clean receipts where goods are in doubtful condition.
3. When delivery is made by Container, to ensure that the Container and its seals are examined immediately by their responsible official.
   If the Container is delivered damaged or with seals broken or missing or with seals other than as stated in the shipping documents, to clause the delivery receipt accordingly and retain all defective or irregular seals for subsequent identification.
4. To apply immediately for survey by Carriers' or other Bailees' Representatives if any loss or damage be apparent and claim on the Carriers or other Bailees for any actual loss or damage found at such survey.
5. To give notice in writing to the Carriers or other Bailees within 3 days of delivery if the loss or damage was not apparent at the time of taking delivery.

NOTE.—The Consignees or their Agents are recommended to make themselves familiar with the Regulations of the Port Authorities at the port of discharge.

SURVEY

In the event of loss or damage which may result in a claim under this Insurance, immediate notice should be given to the Lloyd's Agent at the port or place where the loss or damage is discovered in order that he may examine the goods and issue a survey report.

DOCUMENTATION OF CLAIMS

To enable claims to be dealt with promptly, the Assured or their Agents are advised to submit all available supporting documents without delay, including when applicable:—

1. Original policy or certificate of insurance.
2. Original or copy shipping invoices, together with shipping specification and/or weight notes.
3. Original Bill of Lading and/or other contract of carriage.
4. Survey report or other documentary evidence to show the extent of the loss or damage.
5. Landing account and weight notes at final destination.
6. Correspondence exchanged with the Carriers and other Parties regarding their liability for the loss or damage.

L.P.O. 129A   1.11.76.

Liability Insert

4/1/63

INSTITUTE CARGO CLAUSES (ALL RISKS).

1   1. This insurance attaches from the time the goods leave the warehouse or place of storage at the place named in   Transit
2 the policy for the commencement of the transit, continues during the ordinary course of transit and terminates either on   Clause (in-
3 delivery   corporating
                                                               Warehouse to
4   (a) to the Consignees' or other final warehouse or place of storage at the destination named in   Warehouse
5   the policy,   Clause).
6   (b) to any other warehouse or place of storage, whether prior to or at the destination named
7   in the policy, which the Assured elect to use either
8   (i) for storage other than in the ordinary course of transit
9   or
10   (ii) for allocation or distribution,
11   or (c) on the expiry of 60 days after completion of discharge overside of the goods hereby insured
12   from the oversea vessel at the final port of discharge,
13   whichever shall first occur.

14   If, after discharge overside from the oversea vessel at the final port of discharge, but prior to termination of this
15 insurance, the goods are to be forwarded to a destination other than that to which they are insured hereunder, this insur-
16 ance whilst remaining subject to termination as provided for above, shall not extend beyond the commencement of transit   N/A
17 to such other destination.
18   This insurance shall remain in force (subject to termination as provided for above and to the provisions of Clause 2
19 below) during delay beyond the control of the Assured, any deviation, forced discharge, reshipment or transhipment and
20 during any variation of the adventure arising from the exercise of a liberty granted to shipowners or charterers under the   ✓
21 contract of affreightment.

22   2. If owing to circumstances beyond the control of the Assured either the contract of affreightment is terminated   Termination
23 at a port or place other than the destination named therein or the adventure is otherwise terminated before delivery   of Adventure
24 of the goods as provided for in Clause 1 above, then, subject to prompt notice being given to Underwriters and to an   Clause.
25 additional premium if required, this insurance shall remain in force until either
26   (i) the goods are sold and delivered at such port or place, or, unless otherwise specially agreed, until the
27   expiry of 60 days after completion of discharge overside of the goods hereby insured from the oversea
28   vessel at such port or place, whichever shall first occur,
29   or (ii) if the goods are forwarded within the said period of 60 days (or any agreed extension thereof) to the destin-
30   ation named in the policy or to any other destination until terminated in accordance with the provisions
31   of Clause 1 above.

32   3. Including transit by craft raft or lighter to or from the vessel. Each craft raft or lighter to be deemed a separate   Craft. &c.
33 insurance. The Assured are not to be prejudiced by any agreement exempting lightermen from liability.   Clause.

34   4. Held covered at a premium to be arranged in case of change of voyage or of any omission or error in the descrip-   Change of
35 tion of the interest vessel or voyage.   Voyage Clause

36   5. This insurance is against all risks of loss of or damage to the subject-matter insured but shall in no case be deemed   All Risks
37 to extend to cover loss damage or expense proximately caused by delay or inherent vice or nature of the subject-matter   Clause.
38 insured. Claims recoverable hereunder shall be payable irrespective of percentage.

39   6. No claim for Constructive Total Loss shall be recoverable hereunder unless the goods are reasonably abandoned   Constructive
40 either on account of their actual total loss appearing to be unavoidable or because the cost of recovering, reconditioning   Total Loss
41 and forwarding the goods to the destination to which they are insured would exceed their value on arrival.   Clause.

42   7. General Average and Salvage Charges payable according to Foreign Statement or to York-Antwerp Rules if in   G.A. Clause.
43 accordance with the contract of affreightment.

44   8. The seaworthiness of the vessel as between the Assured and Underwriters is hereby admitted.   Seaworthiness
45   In the event of loss the Assured's right of recovery hereunder shall not be prejudiced by the fact that the loss   Admitted
46 may have been attributable to the wrongful act or misconduct of the shipowners or their servants, committed without   Clause.
47 the privity of the Assured.

48   9. It is the duty of the Assured and their Agents, in all cases, to take such measures as may be reasonable for the   Bailee
49 purpose of averting or minimising a loss and to ensure that all rights against carriers, bailees or other third parties are   Clause.
50 properly preserved and exercised.

51   10. This insurance shall not inure to the benefit of the carrier or other bailee.   Not to Inure
                                                                                              Clause.

52   11. This insurance is extended to indemnify the Assured against such proportion of liability under the contract   " Both to
53 of affreightment " Both to Blame Collision " Clause as is in respect of a loss recoverable hereunder.   Blame
54   In the event of any claim by shipowners under the said Clause the Assured agree to notify the Underwriters   Collision "
55 who shall have the right, at their own cost and expense, to defend the Assured against such claim.   Clause.

56   12. Warranted free of capture, seizure, arrest, restraint and detainment, and the consequences thereof or of any   F.C. & S.
57 attempt thereat ; also from the consequences of hostilities or warlike operations, whether there be a declaration of war   Clause.
58 or not ; but this warranty shall not exclude collision, contact ~~DELETED~~ fixed or floating object (other than a mine or
59 torpedo), stranding, heavy weather or fire unless caused directly and independently of the nature of the voyage or service
60 which the vessel concerned or, in the case of a collision, any other vessel involved therein, is performing) by a hostile act
61 by or against a belligerent power ; and for the purpose of this warranty " power " includes any authority maintaining
62 naval, military or air forces in association with a power.
63   Further warranted free from the consequences of civil war, revolution, rebellion, insurrection, or civil strife
64 arising therefrom, or piracy.
65   Should Clause No. 12 be deleted, the relevant current Institute War Clauses shall be deemed to form part of this
66   insurance.

67   13. Warranted free of loss or damage   F.S.R. & C.C.
68   (a) caused by strikers, locked-out workmen, or persons ~~DELETED~~ taking part in labour disturbances, riots or civil com-   Clause.
69   motions ;
70   (b) resulting from strikes, lock-outs, labour disturbances, riots or civil commotions.
71   Should Clause No. 13 be deleted, the relevant current Institute Strikes Riots and Civil Commotions Clauses shall
72   be deemed to form part of this insurance.

73   14. It is a condition of this insurance that the Assured shall act with reasonable despatch in all circumstances within   Reasonable
74 their control.   Despatch
                                                                                              Clause.

NOTE.—It is necessary for the Assured when they become aware of an event which is " held covered " under this insurance
        to give prompt notice to Underwriters and the right to such cover is dependent upon compliance with this obligation.

CL. 80.   *Sold by Witherby & Co. Ltd., London, E.C.4*   PRINTED IN ENGLAND

Cargo Clauses

INSTITUTE WAR CLAUSES (CARGO)

1. This insurance covers [1]

1.1 the risks excluded from the Standard Form of English Marine Policy by the clause [2]
"Warranted free of capture, seizure, arrest, restraint or detainment, and the consequences thereof [3]
or of any attempt thereat; also from the consequences of hostilities or warlike operations, whether [4]
there be a declaration of war or not; but this warranty shall not exclude collision, contact with any [5]
fixed or floating object (other than a mine or torpedo), stranding, heavy weather or fire unless [6]
caused directly (and independently of the nature of the voyage or service which the vessel concerned [7]
or, in the case of a collision, any other vessel involved therein, is performing) by a hostile act by or [8]
against a belligerent power; and for the purpose of this warranty 'power' includes any authority [9]
maintaining naval, military or air forces in association with a power. [10]
Further warranted free from the consequences of civil war, revolution, rebellion, insurrection, or [11]
civil strife arising therefrom, or piracy." [12]

1.2 loss of or damage to the interest insured caused by [13]

1.2.1 hostilities, warlike operations, civil war, revolution, rebellion, insurrection or civil strife arising [14]
therefrom [15]

1.2.2 mines, torpedoes, bombs or other engines of war [16]

1.3 general average and salvage charges incurred for the purpose of avoiding, or in connection with the [17]
avoidance of, loss by a peril insured against by these clauses. General average and salvage charges [18]
payable according to Foreign Statement or to York-Antwerp Rules if in accordance with the [19]
contract of affreightment. [20]

2. This insurance excludes [21]

2.1 any claim based upon loss of, or frustration of, the insured voyage or adventure caused by arrests [22]
restraints or detainments of Kings Princes Peoples Usurpers or persons attempting to usurp power [23]

2.2 loss damage or expense arising from any hostile use of any weapon of war employing atomic or [24]
nuclear fission and/or fusion or other like reaction or radio-active force or matter [25]

2.3 loss or damage covered by the Standard Form of English Marine Policy with the Free of Capture [26]
etc. Clause (as quoted in 1.1 above) inserted therein [27]

2.4 loss or damage proximately caused by delay inherent vice or loss of market, or any claim for [28]
expenses arising from delay except such expenses as would be recoverable in principle in English law [29]
and practice under York-Antwerp Rules. [30]

3. Claims recoverable shall be payable irrespective of percentage. [31]

4. This insurance, except for the risks of mines and derelict torpedoes, floating or submerged, referred to in [32]
Clause 5 below, [33]

4.1 attaches only as the interest insured and as to any part as that part is loaded on an oversea vessel and [34]

4.2 terminates, subject to 4.5 and 4.6 below, either as the interest and as to any part as that part is [35]
discharged from an oversea vessel at the final port or place of discharge, [36]

or [37]

on expiry of 15 days counting from midnight of the day of arrival of the vessel at the final port or [38]
place of discharge, [39]

whichever shall first occur; [40]

nevertheless, [41]
subject to prompt notice to the Underwriters and to an additional premium, such insurance [42]

4.3 reattaches when, without having discharged the interest at the final port or place of discharge, the [43]
vessel sails therefrom, and [44]

4.4 terminates, subject to 4.5 and 4.6 below, either as the interest and as to any part as that part is [45]
thereafter discharged from the vessel at the final (or substituted) port or place of discharge, [46]

or [47]

on expiry of 15 days counting from midnight of the day of re-arrival of the vessel at the final port or [48]
place of discharge or arrival of the vessel at a substituted port or place of discharge, [49]

whichever shall first occur. [50]

4.5 If during the insured voyage the oversea vessel arrives at an intermediate port or place to discharge [51]
the interest for on-carriage by another oversea vessel, such insurance terminates on expiry of 15 days [52]
counting from midnight of the day of arrival of the vessel at the intermediate port or place, but [53]
reattaches as the interest and as to any part as that part is loaded on the on-carrying oversea vessel. [54]
During the period of 15 days such insurance remains in force after discharge only whilst the interest [55]
and as to any part as that part is at such intermediate port or place of discharge. If the insurance [56]
reattaches, it thereafter terminates in accordance with 4.2. [57]

4.6 If the voyage in the contract of carriage is terminated at a port or place other than the destination [58]
agreed therein, such port or place shall be deemed the final port of discharge and such insurance [59]
terminates in accordance with 4.2. If the interest is subsequently reshipped to the original or any [60]
other destination, then, *provided notice is given to the Underwriters before the* [61]
commencement of such further transit and subject to an additional premium, such insurance [62]
reattaches [63]

4.6.1 in the case of the interest having been discharged, as the interest and as to any part as that part is [64]
loaded on the on-carrying oversea vessel for the voyage; [65]

4.6.2 in the case of the interest not having been discharged, when the vessel sails from such deemed final [66]
port of discharge; [67]

thereafter such insurance terminates in accordance with 4.4. [68]

War Clauses

on expiry of 15 days counting from midnight of the day of re-arrival of the vessel at the final port or 48
place of discharge or arrival of the vessel at a substituted port or place of discharge, 49
whichever shall first occur. 50

4.5 If during the insured voyage the oversea vessel arrives at an intermediate port or place to discharge 51
the interest for on-carriage by another oversea vessel, such insurance terminates on expiry of 15 days 52
counting from midnight of the day of arrival of the vessel at the intermediate port or place, but 53
reattaches as the interest and as to any part as that part is loaded on the on-carrying oversea vessel. 54
During the period of 15 days such insurance remains in force after discharge only whilst the interest 55
and as to any part as that part is at such intermediate port or place of discharge. If the insurance 56
reattaches, it thereafter terminates in accordance with 4.2. 57

4.6 If the voyage in the contract of carriage is terminated at a port or place other than the destination 58
agreed therein, such port or place shall be deemed the final port of discharge and such insurance 59
terminates in accordance with 4.2. If the interest is subsequently reshipped to the original or any 60
other destination, then, *provided notice is given to the Underwriters before the* 61
commencement of such further transit and subject to an additional premium, such insurance 62
reattaches 63

4.6.1 in the case of the interest having been discharged, as the interest and as to any part as that part is 64
loaded on the on-carrying oversea vessel for the voyage; 65

4.6.2 in the case of the interest not having been discharged, when the vessel sails from such deemed final 66
port of discharge; 67

thereafter such insurance terminates in accordance with 4.4. 68

(For the purpose of Clause 4 69
"arrival" shall be deemed to mean that the vessel is anchored, moored or otherwise secured at a berth or place 70
within the Harbour Authority area. If such a berth or place is not available, arrival is deemed to have 71
occurred when the vessel first anchors, moors or otherwise secures either at or off the intended port or place 72
of discharge) 73

5. The insurance against the risks of mines and derelict torpedoes, floating or submerged, 74

5.1 attaches as the interest and as to any part as that part is first loaded on vessel or craft after such 75
interest leaves the warehouse or place of storage at the place named in the insurance for the 76
commencement of the transit and 77

5.2 terminates either 78

5.2.1 as the interest and as to any part as that part is discharged finally from vessel or craft prior 79
to delivery to the warehouse or place of storage at the destination named in the insurance, or at 80
a substituted destination in the event of a change of voyage agreed to by the Underwriters, 81
or, 82

5.2.2 when, before the interest is discharged finally from vessel or craft prior to delivery to the 83
warehouse or place of storage at the destination named in the insurance, or at a substituted 84
destination in the event of a change of voyage agreed to by the Underwriters, the voyage or 85
transit in the contract of carriage is terminated at a port or place other than the destination 86
agreed therein; nevertheless, *subject to prompt notice to the Underwriters and to an additional* 87
premium if required, such insurance reattaches, and thereafter terminates either 88

5.2.2.1 as the interest and as to any part as that part is discharged from vessel or craft prior to sale 89
and delivery at such port or place 90
or, 91

5.2.2.2 unless otherwise specially agreed by the Underwriters, on the expiry of 60 days whilst 92
afloat after completion of discharge overside of the interest from an oversea vessel at such 93
port or place, 94

whichever shall first occur. 95

If the interest is forwarded within the 60 days (or any agreed extension thereof) to the 96
destination named in the insurance or to any other destination, then, *subject to prompt* 97
notice to the Underwriters and to an additional premium, such insurance remains in force 98
until terminated as the interest and as to any part as that part is discharged finally from 99
vessel or craft prior to delivery to the warehouse or place of storage at the destination 100
named in the insurance, or at a substituted destination in the event of a change of voyage 101
agreed to by the Underwriters. 102

(For the purpose of Clause 4 and Clause 5 103
"oversea vessel" shall be deemed to mean a vessel carrying the interest from one port or place to another 104
where such voyage involves a sea passage by that vessel) 105

6. **Anything contained in this contract which is inconsistent with Clauses 2.1, 2.2, 4 or 5 shall, to the extent** 106
of such inconsistency, be null and void. 107

7. *Subject to prompt notice to the Underwriters and to an additional premium,* the interest is held covered 108
within the provisions of these clauses in the case of 109

7.1 change of or deviation from the voyage 110

7.2 variation of the adventure by reason of the exercise of any liberty granted to the shipowner or 111
charterer under the contract of affreightment. 112

8. **It is a condition of this insurance that the Assured shall act with reasonable despatch in all circumstances** 113
within their control. 114

CL 27. *Sold by Witherby & Co. Ltd., London.*

War Clauses

INSTITUTE STRIKES RIOTS AND CIVIL COMMOTIONS CLAUSES.

1. This insurance covers loss of or damage to the property hereby insured caused by   1

    (a) strikers, locked-out workmen, or persons taking part in labour disturbances, riots or civil commotions;   2

    (b) persons acting maliciously.   3

2. Warranted free of   4

    (i) loss or damage proximately caused by   5

        (a) delay, inherent vice or nature of the property hereby insured;   6

        (b) the absence, shortage or withholding of labour of any description whatsoever during any strike, lock   7
out, labour disturbance, riot or civil commotion;   8

    (ii) any claim for expenses arising from delay except such expenses as would be recoverable in principle   9
in English law and practice under York-Antwerp Rules, 1950;   10

    (iii) loss or damage caused by hostilities warlike operations civil war, or by revolution rebellion insurrection   11
or civil strife arising therefrom.   12

3. This insurance attaches from the time the goods leave the warehouse or place of storage at the place named in   13
the policy for the commencement of the transit, continues during the ordinary course of transit and terminates either on   14
delivery   15

    (a) to the Consignees' or other final warehouse or place of storage at the destination named in   16
the policy,   17

    (b) to any other warehouse or place of storage, whether prior to or at the destination named   18
in the policy, which the Assured elect to use either   19

        (i) for storage other than in the ordinary course of transit   20
        or   21
        (ii) for allocation or distribution,   22

or (c) on the expiry of 60 days after completion of discharge overside of the goods hereby insured   23
from the oversea vessel at the final port of discharge,   24

    whichever shall first occur.   25

If, after discharge overside from the oversea vessel at the final port of discharge, but prior to termination of this   26
insurance, the goods are to be forwarded to a destination other than that to which they are insured hereunder, this insur-   27
ance whilst remaining subject to termination as provided for above, shall not extend beyond the commencement of transit   28
to such other destination.   29

This insurance shall remain in force (subject to termination as provided for above and to the provisions of Clause 4   30
below) during delay beyond the control of the Assured, any deviation, forced discharge, reshipment or transhipment and   31
during any variation of the adventure arising from the exercise of a liberty granted to shipowners or charterers under the   32
contract of affreightment.   33

4. If owing to circumstances beyond the control of the Assured either the contract of affreightment is terminated   34
at a port or place other than the destination named therein or the adventure is otherwise terminated before delivery   35
of the goods as provided for in Clause 3 above, then, subject to prompt notice being given to Underwriters and to an   36
additional premium if required, this insurance shall remain in force until either   37

    (i) the goods are sold and delivered at such port or place, or, unless otherwise specially agreed, until the   38
expiry of 60 days after completion of discharge overside of the goods hereby insured from the oversea   39
vessel at such port or place, whichever shall first occur,   40

or (ii) if the goods are forwarded within the said period of 60 days (or any agreed extension thereof) to the destin-   41
ation named in the policy or to any other destination, until terminated in accordance with the provisions   42
of Clause 3 above.   43

5. General Average and Salvage Charges payable (subject to the terms of these clauses) according to Foreign State-   44
ment or York-Antwerp Rules if in accordance with the contract of affreightment.   45

6. Claims for loss or damage within the terms of these clauses shall be payable without reference to conditions of   46
average.   47

7. Held covered at a premium to be arranged in case of change of voyage or of any omission or error in the descrip-   48
tion of the interest vessel or voyage.   49

8. It is a condition of this insurance that the Assured shall act with reasonable despatch in all circumstances within   50
their control.   51

NOTE.—It is necessary for the Assured when they become aware of an event which is "held covered" under this insurance
to give prompt notice to Underwriters and the right to such cover is dependent upon compliance with this obligation.

CL. 109.   Sold by Witherby & Co Ltd., London.   PRINTED IN ENGLAND.

Civil Commotions Clauses

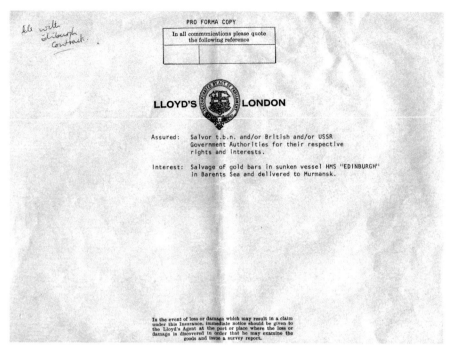

PRO FORMA COPY

In all communications please quote
the following reference

LLOYD'S LONDON

Assured: Salvor t.b.n. and/or British and/or USSR
Government Authorities for their respective
rights and interests.

Interest: Salvage of gold bars in sunken vessel HMS "EDINBURGH"
in Barents Sea and delivered to Murmansk.

In the event of loss or damage which may result in a claim
under this Insurance, immediate notice should be given to
the Lloyd's Agent at the port or place where the loss or
damage is discovered in order that he may examine the
goods and issue a survey report.

PRO FORMA COPY

No Policy or other Contract dated on or after 1st Jan., 1924, will be recognised by the Committee of Lloyd's
as entitling the holder to the benefit of the Funds and/or Guarantees lodged by the Underwriters of the
Policy or Contract as security for their liabilities unless it bears at foot the Seal of Lloyd's Policy Signing Office.

Be it known that   AS ATTACHED

as well in   *their*   own name as for and in the name and names of all and every other person or persons
to whom the same doth, may, or shall appertain, in part or in all, doth make assurance and cause   *themselves*
and them, and every of them, to be insured, lost or not lost, at and from

AS ATTACHED

Upon any kind of goods and merchandises, and also upon the body, tackle, apparel, ordnance, munition, artillery,
boat, and other furniture, of and in the good ship or vessel called the

AS ATTACHED

whereof is master under God, for this present voyage, or whosoever else shall go for master in the said ship, or by
whatsoever other name or names the same ship, or the master thereof, is or shall be named or called ; beginning
the adventure upon the said goods and merchandises from the loading thereof aboard the said ship, *as above*
upon the said ship, &c., *as above* and so shall continue and endure, during her abode there, upon the said ship,
&c. And further, until the said ship, with all her ordnance, tackle, apparel, &c., and goods and merchandises
whatsoever shall be arrived at *as above* upon the said ship, &c., until she hath moored at anchor twenty-four
hours in good safety ; and upon the goods and merchandises, until the same be there discharged and safely
landed. And it shall be lawful for the said ship, &c., in this voyage, to proceed and sail to and touch and
stay at any ports or places whatsoever *and wheresoever for all purposes* without prejudice to this insurance.
The said ship, &c., goods and merchandises, &c., for so much as concerns the assured by agreement between
the assured and assurers in this policy, are and shall be valued at

AS ATTACHED

(No.   )

S.G.

Any person not an Underwriting Member
of Lloyd's subscribing this Policy, or any person
uttering the same if so subscribed, will be liable
to be proceeded against under Lloyd's Acts.

£ 50,000,000 in all.

Printed at Lloyd's, London, England.

INSTITUTE DANGEROUS DRUGS CLAUSE.
"It is understood and agreed that no claim under this
Policy will be paid in respect of drugs to which the
various International Conventions relating to Opium
and other dangerous drugs apply unless
  (1) the drugs shall be expressly declared as such in
      the Policy and the name of the country from
      which, and the name of the country to which
      they are consigned shall be specifically stated in
      the Policy
                        and
  (2) the proof of loss is accompanied either by a licence,
      certificate or authorisation issued by the Govern-
      ment of the country to which the drugs are
      consigned showing that the importation of the
      consignment into that country has been approved
      by that Government, or, alternatively, by a
      licence, certificate or authorisation issued by
      the Government of the country from which the
      drugs are consigned showing that the export of
      the consignment to the destination stated has been
      approved by that Government;
                        and
  (3) the route by which the drugs were conveyed
      was usual and customary."

Lloyds Policy Cover (top) and Rear (bottom)

APPENDIX 4

The pages within this appendix are copies of various documents which were used in accounting the gold and salvage agreements.

BANK OF ENGLAND.

SCHEDULE OF GOLD BARS.

ACCOUNT

yer.	Series.	Bar. Number.	Oz. Gross.	Assay.	Oz. Fine.
CRWARD		80	30631.500		30628.324
	P	91081	378.225	.9999	378.187
	P	91082	365.525	.9999	365.488
	P	91083	380.425	.9999	380.387
	P	91084	385.025	.9999	384.986
	P	91085	378.325	.9999	378.287
	P	91086	384.725	.9999	384.686
	P	91087	364.025	.9999	363.988
	P	91088	384.625	.9999	384.586
	P	91089	386.050	.9999	386.011
	P	91090	373.300	.9999	373.262
	P	91091	368.100	.9999	368.063
	P	91092	372.575	.9999	372.537
	P	91093	378.775	.9999	370.738
	P	91094	397.975	.9999	397.935
	P	91095	370.500	.9999	370.463
	P	91096	384.725	.9999	384.686
	P	91097	400.000	.9999	399.960
	P	91098	384.925	.9999	384.886
	P	91099	389.050	.9999	389.011
	P	91100	384.900	.9999	384.861
	P	91101	394.700	.9999	394.660
	P	91102	399.050	.9998	398.970
	P	91103	385.025	.9999	384.986
	P	91104	382.575	.9999	382.536
	P	91105	405.425	.9999	405.384
	P	91106	384.625	.9999	384.586
	P	91107	401.900	.9999	401.859
	P	91108	384.550	.9999	384.511
	P	91109	383.975	.9999	383.936
	P	91110	387.425	.9999	387.386
	P	91111	370.150	.9999	370.113
	P	91112	369.625	.9999	369.588
	P	91113	380.325	.9999	380.287
	P	91114	392.200	.9999	392.160
	P	91115	383.625	.9999	383.586
	P	91116	393.825	.9999	393.785
	P	91117	386.000	.9999	385.961
	P	91118	384.800	.9999	384.761
	P	91119	386.550	.9999	386.511
	P	91120	392.075	.9999	392.035
CRWARD		120	45983.700		45978.933

Bank of England Gold Schedules 1

BANK OF ENGLAND.

SCHEDULE OF GOLD BARS.

ACCOUNT _____

yer.	Series.	Bar. Number.	Oz. Gross.	Assay.	Oz. Fine.
RWARD		120	45983.700		45978.933
	P	91121	382.400	.9999	382.361
	P	91122	369.300	.9999	369.263
	P	91123	380.575	.9999	380.537
	P	91124	386.375	.9999	386.336
	P	91125	390.775	.9999	390.736
	P	91126	376.775	.9999	376.737
	P	91127	359.750	.9999	359.714
	P	91128	362.375	.9999	362.338
	P	91129	408.575	.9999	408.534
	P	91130	398.475	.9998	398.395
	P	91131	400.000	.9998	399.920
	P	91132	386.200	.9999	386.161
	P	91133	405.675	.9999	405.634
	P	91134	389.150	.9999	389.111
	P	91135	368.275	.9999	368.238
	P	91136	398.875	.9999	398.835
	P	91137	404.150	.9999	404.109
	P	91138	368.350	.9999	368.313
	P	91139	374.900	.9999	374.862
	P	91140	384.950	.9999	384.911
	P	91141	406.300	.9999	406.259
	P	91142	384.025	.9999	383.986
	P	91143	403.300	.9999	403.259
	P	91144	379.450	.9999	379.412
	P	91145	394.450	.9999	394.410
	P	91146	384.975	.9998	384.898
	P	91147	376.625	.9999	376.587
	P	91148	370.700	.9999	370.663
	P	91149	375.225	.9999	375.187
	P	91150	385.325	.9999	385.286
	P	91151	370.750	.9999	370.713
	P	91152	370.300	.9999	370.263
	P	91153	376.025	.9999	375.987
	P	91154	385.725	.9999	385.686
	P	91155	368.075	.9999	368.038
	P	91156	375.200	.9999	375.162
	P	91157	386.475	.9999	386.436
	P	91158	401.850	.9999	401.809
	P	91159	389.750	.9999	389.711
	P	91160	404.500	.9999	404.459
RWARD		160	61368.625		61362.189

Bank of England Gold Schedules 2

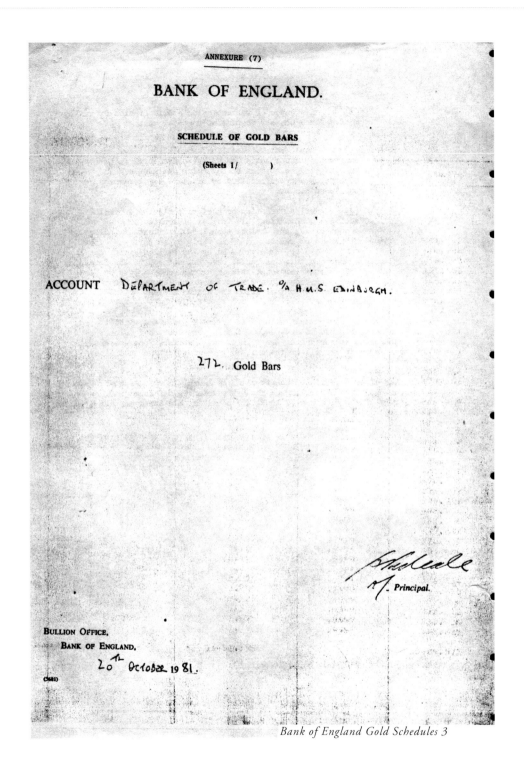

ANNEXURE (7)

BANK OF ENGLAND.

SCHEDULE OF GOLD BARS

(Sheets 1/   )

ACCOUNT   DEPARTMENT OF TRADE. ⁰/ₐ H.M.S. EDINBURGH.

272. Gold Bars

Principal.

BULLION OFFICE,
   BANK OF ENGLAND.
         20ᵗʰ October 1981.

Bank of England Gold Schedules 3

- 2 -

(2)   any weapon of war employing atomic fission or radio-active force whether in time of peace or war;

(3)   insurrection, rebellion, revolution, civil war, usurped power, or action taken by governmental authority in hindering, combating or defending against such an occurrence, or confiscation by order of any government or public authority.

(4)   nuclear reaction or nuclear radiation or radio-active contamination, all whether controlled or uncontrolled, and whether such loss be direct or indirect, proximate or remote, or be in whole or in part caused by, contributed to, or aggravated by the peril(s) insured against in this insurance; however, subject to the foregoing and all provisions of this insurance, direct loss by fire resulting from nuclear reaction or nuclear radiation or radioactive contamination is insured against by this insurance.

This insurance covers only within the United Kingdom and liability hereunder is limited to £25,000,000 for any one loss; but in case of successive losses during the term of the insurance Underwriters are liable for each and all of them, up to the amount of the insurance for each loss.

In case of loss or misfortune it shall be lawful to the Assured to sue, labour, and travel for, in and about the defence, safeguard and recovery of the Property, without prejudice to this insurance and at the expense of Underwriters.

STEWART WRIGHTSON (SURETY & SPECIE) LIMITED

DIRECTOR

COPY

Dated in London......14th October 1981.........

Nuclear Exclusion

Cargo Salvage Agreement 1

Cargo Salvage Agreement 2

ANNEXURE (1)

STA

COLLECTION NOTE

From: **BRINK'S-MAT LTD.**
36-41 HOLYWELL LANE
LONDON EC2P 2EQ.

Telephone: 01-247 9481
Telex: 885292

To: The Secretary of State for Trade
of the United Kingdom

Date: 16 October 1981

Dear Sirs,

Please deliver to the Bearer, Mr. R.D.L. Vaughan-Griffith

111 (One hundred and eleven) bars/boxes/items

said to contain Gold Value £ *10,230,192 : 59* for shipment

for

to Bank of England, Threadneedle Street, London.

Please note that this business is undertaken subject to the Conditions of our Special Trading Agreement, in accordance with your instructions.

Yours faithfully,
BRINK'S-MAT LTD.

Received the above-mentioned .... bars/boxes/items.

"Brink's Mat" Collection Notice

(2) Collection Note from Brink's-Mat Limited to Jessop Marine Recoveries Limited and dated the 16th October 1981

(3) Collection Note from Brink's-Mat Limited to Wharton Williams Limited and dated the 16th October 1981

(4) Collection Note from Brink's-Mat Limited to Offshore Supply Association Limited and dated the 16th October 1981

(5) Collection Note from Brink's-Mat Limited to Racal-Decca Survey Limited and dated the 16th October 1981

(6) Certificate of Insurance dated 14th October 1981

(7) Schedule of 272 gold bars issued by the Bank of England and dated 20th October 1981

(8) Schedule of 3 gold bars dated 20th October 1981 - Racal-Decca Survey Limited

(9) Schedule of 13 gold bars dated 20th October 1981 - Jessop Marine Recoveries Limited

(10) Schedule of 48 gold bars dated 20th October 1981 - Wharton Williams Limited

(11) Schedule of 97 gold bars dated 20th October 1981 - Offshore Supply Association Limited

(12) Schedule of 111 gold bars dated 20th October 1981 - The Secretary of State for Trade of the United Kingdom

"Brink's Mat" Schedule

APPENDIX 5

The pages within this appendix are copies of documents outlining the security procedures we followed in order to ensure safe accounting and delivery of the recovered gold.

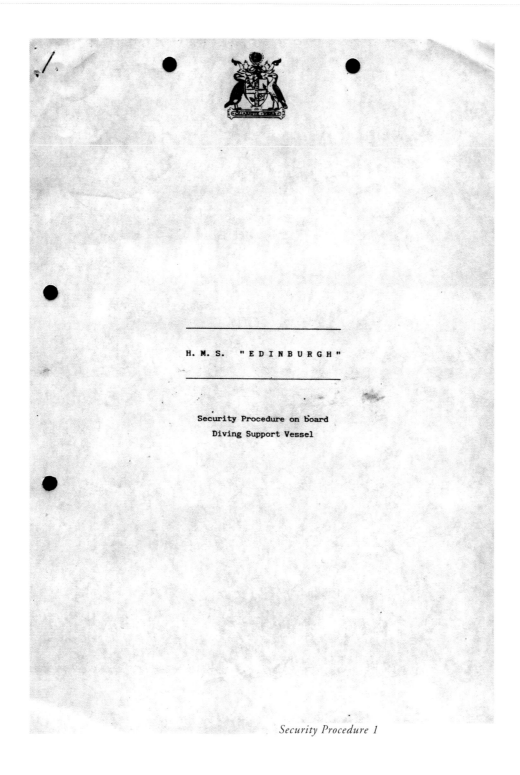

H. M. S. "E D I N B U R G H"

Security Procedure on board
Diving Support Vessel

Security Procedure 1

Page 1

H. M. S. " E D I N B U R G H "

****

<u>On Board Security Procedure</u>

The following security procedure and ancillary arrangements are to be closely followed at all times for the safe custody of any gold ingots recovered from the Wreck of H.M.S. "Edinburgh" ("the Wreck") and taken aboard the Diving Support Recovery Vessel (D.S.R.V.).

<u>1.00</u> <u>All</u> references to clauses below are to the clauses of the Salvage Agreement dated 18th July 1986("the Salvage Agreement")

between

The Insurance Company of the U.S.S.R. (Ingosstrakh) Limited ("the Soviet Principal")

and

The Secretary of State for Transport of the United Kingdom ("the British Principal")

and

Jessop Marine Recoveries Limited ("JMRL")

<u>2.00</u> <u>Each</u> ingot recovered from the Wreck will be received on the deck of the D.S.R.V. in the presence of:-

      (a) The nominated representatives of the Soviet Principal ("Representatives S")

      and

      (b) Mr. D.M.D. Keogh and Captain G.C. Belson, the nominated representatives of the British Principal ("Representatives B")

      and

      (c) The nominated representative of JMRL ("Representative C")

Security Procedure 2

Page 2

3.00 Captain G.C. Belson will also act as the nominated representative of The Salvage Association

4.00 Each ingot received on the deck of the D.S.R.V. will be washed, and carefully scrubbed clean, with a soft bristle brush, of any marine growth. However, this procedure will only be intended to be an initial cleaning operation, and no foreign metal fragments will be removed at this stage, nor will any ingots that may be joined together be prised apart, or any type of cutting operation be carried out on an ingot

5.00 An initial note will be made by each of the Representatives of each ingot received on the deck of the D.S.R.V.

6.00 Each ingot received on the deck of the D.S.R.V. will, after careful cleaning, be taken below and re-checked by each Representative upon its arrival in the strongroom compartment in which the ingots are to be stowed

7.00 Once an ingot is received within the strongroom compartment, Captain Belson will take four colour Polaroid phtographs of the ingot, one for Representative S, one for the British Principal, one for Representative C, and one for The Salvage Association. This will then provide the appropriate permanent record for the Soviet Principal, the British Principal, and JMRL. The measurements of each ingot and the weight stamped thereon will then be recorded in quadruplicate on the forms provided for that purpose by The Salvage Assocition. Each form is numbered consecutively commencing at 100. The forms will then be signed by each Representative and copies distributed as indicated on the forms (copy attached)

8.00 The door to the strongroom compartment will be fitted with three separate padlocks, all of which will have two keys

9.00 The padlocks will be provided by The Salvage Association

Security Procedure 3

Page 3

10.00   The keys for each of the padlocks will be distributed as follows:-

Padlock No. 1
Key No 1 will be in the possession of Captain G.C. Belson
Key No. 2 will be deposited with The Salvage Association in London
Padlock No. 2
Key No. 3 will be in the possession of the Master of the D.S.R.V.
Key No. 4 will be deposited with The Salvage Association in London
Padlock No. 3
Key No. 5 will be in the possession of Representative C
Key No. 6 will be deposited with The Salvage Association in London

11.00   The door to the strongroom compartment will be kept locked at all times

12.00   Captain G.C. Belson will be responsible for carrying out "Uncertain Musters" of the ingots within the strongroom compartment, in the presence of Representative C, the Master of the D.S.R.V. and Representatives S (should they wish to be present), at intervals between musters not exceeding twenty four hours. These musters will continue until final discharge of all cargo

13.00   Captain G.C. Belson will also be responsible for keeping a written record of all "Musters", and the movements of any ingots in and out of the strongroom compartment

14.00   Upon completion of the recovery, the division of the ingots recovered will then take place pursuant to Clause 22

Security Procedure 4

Page 4

15.00 <u>Pursuant</u> to Clause 22 (2) a statement in quadruplicate is to be made of the markings, measurements and weights of the ingots apportioned to each Principal utilising the forms described in Paragraph 7.00 of this Security Procedure. Each form will be completed in English, and signed by each of the nominated Representatives of the Soviet Principal, the British Principal and JMRL, signifying agreement to the apportionment. The Soviet Principal's nominated Representatives, on taking custody of the ingots apportioned to their Principal, are then to sign the aforementioned forms officially acknowledging receipt from the Contractor of the ingots apportioned to them

16.00 <u>The</u> Soviet Principal's nominated Representatives will then be responsible for the supervision and unloading of the ingots apportioned to the Soviet Principal pursuant to Clause 22

17.00 <u>Captain</u> G.C. Belson will sign the British Principal's and JMRL's copy of the statement referred to in paragraph 15.00 above, to acknowledge the presence of the remaining ingots within the strongroom compartment

18.00 <u>The</u> D.S.R.V. wil then proceed to Aberdeen to discharge the British Principal's proportion of the Cargo

19.00 <u>Once</u> the D.S.R.V. has come alongside in Aberdeen the British Principal's nominated Representatives will acknowledge receipt of the Cargo apportioned to the British Principal on the forms and in the manner described in Paragraph 15.00 above

20.00 <u>Upon</u> final discharge of the Cargo the three padlocks and three keys will be returned to Captain G.C. Belson

****

Security Procedure 5

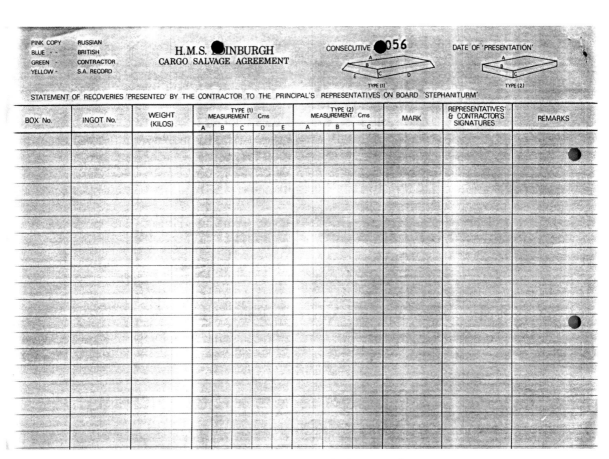

Blank Cargo Salvage Agreement Form

ACKNOWLEDGEMENTS

Malcolm Williams and I owe a great debt to many dedicated people who made this record-breaking salvage possible. I cannot list everybody involved, but would like to thank the following in particular:

Mike Stewart and John Clarke, whose professionalism and attention to detail made the project succeed.

Mike O'Meara and his two supervisors, Derrick Hesketh and Dave Keen. Between them, they carried the direct responsibility for the lives of the divers. That is a heavy responsibility to bear and they bore it and completed the deepest diving salvage ever without any serious incidents.

The diving crew who actually put their lives on the line, venturing into new territory. As a diver myself, albeit a shallow-water diver, I can really appreciate the fear and apprehension that they cheerfully and successfully faced.

Ronnie Goetz and his crew handled the *Stephaniturm* impeccably. Without their professionalism we could not have succeeded.

David Keogh and the Salvage Association were professional and honest at all times and really helped the project succeed.

Without Keith Jessop's idea and original research work, the salvage would never have occurred.

My long-suffering wife Jackie put up with my long absences and eventually forgave me for putting her home on the line without telling her.

My final thoughts are for the mean, greedy, venal, jealous, and dishonest British Government and Civil Service. Their behaviour in this project is symptomatic of how they have taken the "Great" out of "Great Britain." I would advise anyone considering a salvage operation to conduct the operation from outside Britain. I myself would never base a salvage operation here again.

REFERENCES

1) "The Funnel of Gold" by Mendel Peterson published by Little Brown and Company.

2) "The Wreck of the Almiranta" by Peter Earle published by McMillan.

3) "The Log of the *Centurion*" by Leo Heaps published by book Club Associates London.

4) "Stalin's Gold" by Barrie Penrose published by Grenada (withdrawn from circulation).

5) "Treasures of the Armada" by Robert Stenuit published by David and Charles.

6) "The Egypt's Gold" by David Scott published by Faber and Faber.

7) "Shipwrecks in the Americas" by Robert Marx published by Dover Publications.

8) "The Tobermory Treasure" by Alison McLeay published by Conway Maritime Press.

9) "Undersea Treasures" by the National Geographical Society.

10) "L'Or de Staline" by Patrick Mouton published by Pen Duick.

11) "The Russian Convoys" by B.B. Schofield published by Pan.

12) "The Second World War" by Winston Churchill published by Cassel.

BIOGRAPHY

Ric Wharton worked as a civil engineer from 1964 to 1970 specialising in lifeboat stations, harbour and coastal works and maritime engineering.

After learning to dive in 1960, Mr. Wharton entered the diving industry in 1970 working in the Persian Gulf and the Gulf of Mexico before joining the French company Comex as managing director of their North Sea Operations.

Having built up the Comex operations in the North Sea, he formed Wharton Williams Ltd. (2W) which soon became one of the largest diving companies in the world.

In 1981 Mr. Wharton led 2W in the world record-breaking salvage of £50,000,000 of gold bullion from the wreck of the cruiser HMS *Edinburgh* at 256 metres (840 feet) in the Barents Sea.

Mr.Wharton sold 2W in 1989 and has since set up his own group of small offshore companies based in Aberdeen, Scotland.